THE *VANITY FAIR* LITHOGRAPHS

GARLAND REFERENCE LIBRARY
OF THE HUMANITIES
(VOL. 120)

THE VANITY FAIR LITHOGRAPHS
An Illustrated Checklist

Jerold Savory

Photography by Tom Poland

GARLAND PUBLISHING, INC. • NEW YORK & LONDON
1978

Library of Congress Cataloging in Publication Data

Savory, Jerold.
 The Vanity fair lithographs.

 (Garland reference library of the humanities; v. 120)
 Bibliography: p.
 Includes index.
 1. Lithography—19th century—Catalogs.
 2. Lithography—20th century—Catalogs. 3. Vanity fair
 (London). I. Title.
 NE2297.S38   741.5'909'034   78-104
 ISBN 0-8240-9824-2

Printed on acid-free, 250-year-life paper
Manufactured in the United States of America

For Vera Hinkle
And in memory of Walter

CONTENTS

ACKNOWLEDGMENTS

I would like to thank the following collectors and/or print dealers for loaning prints for photographs: Thomas S. Benjamin and Vanity Fair, Ltd., Robert Felix, Michael Griffin, William McLeod, William Mitchell, Dr. Robert Moxon, Kenneth Taylor and Westwood's La Belle Epoque, and Ernest Trubiano. Also appreciated have been advice and encouragement from John Mebane, Editor of *The Antiques Journal.* Hobart F. Berolzheimer and the staff of The Free Library of Philadelphia deserve credit for helping to make available to me a nearly complete collection of *Vanity Fair* magazines for purposes of checking names and dates. Tom Poland and I thank the J. Drake Edens Library of Columbia College, South Carolina, for the use of equipment and facilities in preparing the photographs. Finally, thanks to Dot Knight for her secretarial skills and to my family for their interest and patience.

INTRODUCTION
Vanity Fair: 1868–1914

This Checklist has been prepared in response to the increasing popularity of the delightful gallery of some two thousand drawings of colorful personalities that were published in the British *Vanity Fair* from 1869 to 1914. My purpose is to provide a chronological checklist of these drawings, indexed alphabetically and accompanied by selected illustrations. Based largely upon the system of reference notes I have devised during the past ten years as a collector, the book will, I hope, be a useful reference for others interested in researching and/or collecting the prints. Those interested in information beyond the scope of this necessarily brief introduction may want to consult works listed in the bibliography.

The story of *Vanity Fair* revolves principally around the talents and personalities of three men: the founding editor, Thomas Gibson Bowles (Figs. 61 and 109), and the two major artists of the caricatures, Carlo Pellegrini (Fig. 60) and Sir Leslie Ward (Fig. 63).

Thomas Gibson Bowles (1842–1922)

Despite the more abiding and universal appeal of the "cartoons" (as they were originally called), Bowles' "letter-press" commentaries accompanying each drawing provide amusing literary supplements to the art. Under various sobriquets, Bowles wrote most of the magazine's material, including the biographical sketches under the name "Jehu Junior," during his ownership of the magazine from 1868 to 1889. Other editors were O.A. Fry, from 1889 to 1904, and Frank Harris, from 1904 to 1913. Later writers continued to use the "Jehu Junior" signature, but they did not match Bowles' own terse and clever comments and his often caustic wit.

Born the illegitimate son of Susan Bowles and Thomas Milner Gibson, Thomas Gibson Bowles was raised in the household of Gibson and his wife, Arethusa, a remarkably broad-minded woman whose salons provided him with regular contacts among the English social set he was later to satirize in his magazine. On November 7, 1868, he introduced his first issue:

> In this Show it is proposed to display the vanities of the week, without ignoring or disguising the fact that they are vanities, but keeping in mind that in the buying and selling of them there is to be made a profit of Truth.

With this stated purpose winding its way into a variety of articles in each issue, *Vanity Fair*'s urbane journalism remains among the best examples of that style of English prose. But journalism alone was insufficient, and by the end of 1868, declining sales indicated that something more was needed.

The answer came in the "lucky" thirteenth issue on January 30, 1869, which contained a full-page colored caricature of Benjamin Disraeli (Fig. 1) signed by "Singe," the pen name for the Italian artist Carlo Pellegrini, who, after his second contribution (Gladstone, Fig. 2), in the following issue, was to sign his familiar "Ape" on hundreds of cartoons for the next fifteen years of *Vanity Fair*'s successful forty-five-year history. With the introduction of the cartoons, the magazine's success was assured. By March, 1869, sales had more than tripled those of the first issue.

Carlo Pellegrini (1839–1889)

Italian-born Pellegrini was a Neapolitan fashion leader who in 1864 came to London, where his humor and personality soon made him the pet of English society as well. Bowles, who likely had met Pellegrini in Arethusa Milner Gibson's salons, knew that he had found the right combination for *Vanity Fair*'s success. Pellegrini was an ingenious caricature artist who had amused socialites of both Naples and London with his thumbnail sketches of their leading personalities, an artistic talent most likely inspired by the *portraits chargés* of Delfico.

Several of Pellegrini's early drawings, especially those of Grant-Duff (Fig. 6), Knatchbull-Hugessen (Fig. 10), and Carlyle (Fig. 11) show how Pellegrini lived up to his pen name, "Ape," by giving "ape-like" characteristics to his subjects. Although Bowles had to defend the cartoons against some who said they were too cruel and grim, many of Pellegrini's drawings are remarkably candid in capturing personality traits of his "victims." Many of the earlier drawings, including several by "Spy" and other artists who worked with Pellegrini during the 1870's, were less flattering than later ones, which were more character portraits than caricatures (see Figs. 90, 96, 98, and 115, for example). But often these earlier drawings, despite their exaggerations, capture both character and actual physical likeness with unusual skill. Compare such cartoons as Figs. 16, 17, and 40 with existing photographs of Darwin, Arnold, and Newman, for example. Furthermore, Bowles' repeated defenses of his artists' work gave rise to some of his most insightful commentary on the social function of caricature satire. His central idea of caricature satire as "the unheroic representation of heroes" is expanded in numerous Prefaces to collected "Albums" of the drawings, published by individual years and special categories in response to growing public demand.

In the 1877 Preface, Bowles announced that "Ape" would be sharing the artistic labors of weekly productions with "Spy," a wise decision for several reasons. During 1874 and 1875, Pellegrini had done *all* of the weekly drawings, a remarkable achievement considering the time involved for each and the fact that subjects were not limited to the more readily available peers, parliamentarians, and politicians in London. They included, as well, the poet Robert Browning (Fig. 36); the actors Henry Irving (Fig. 32), Salvini (Fig. 35), and C.J. Mathews; the American evangelists Dwight L. Moody (Fig. 33) and Ira Sankey (Fig. 34); the scientists Müller and Playfair; and the Channel swimmer Matthew Webb. Also, following this productive period as a caricaturist, Pellegrini temporarily left *Vanity Fair* to pursue other artistic ambitions. Finally, Bowles had a willing and talented fill-in in Leslie Ward, whose "Spy" drawings had filled half the issues of 1873 and nearly all those of 1876 during "Ape's" absence. Although Pellegrini returned in 1877 to continue to contribute for the remaining decade of his life, the great majority of cartoons for the rest of *Vanity Fair*'s history were done by Leslie Ward. Indeed, so closely identified did he become with the magazine that during the twentieth century, *Vanity Fair*'s total collection of more than two thousand drawings is usually referred to simply as "Spy Cartoons."

Sir Leslie Ward (1851–1922)

As a child, Leslie, the son of Royal Academy artist E.M. Ward (Fig. 28) and of a mother who was also a painter, was determined to be an artist. Delighted to make mental sketches of distinguished house guests, he was always drawing and, during his days at Eton, became the school's caricaturist. Influenced no doubt by his father's talents as a portrait painter and caricaturist, Leslie contributed his first drawing to the March 1, 1873, issue of *Vanity Fair*, a delightful caricature of the versatile naturalist and anti-Darwinist Professor Richard Owen (Fig. 25), affectionately known as "Old Bones." His second contribution, of Edward Levy, bore the soon-to-be-famous "Spy" signature, a name he happened to note while opening a Johnson's dictionary.

The "Spy" sobriquet was appropriate for one who would spend hours watching his subjects to catch distinctive impressions before sketching (unlike Pellegrini, who was able to "ape" his victims with immediate precision). "He is a keen sportsman whose quarry is man," said *Vanity Fair* when Ward's own portrait appeared in 1889 (Fig. 63), "and he could tell stories of stalking which would make the most hardened deer-stalker pale with envy." Except for a few contributions to other magazines, Ward spent the remainder of his career as the "Spy" of *Vanity Fair*, only on rare occasions signing either his full name or playfully writing "L. Ward" backwards as "Drawl."

From the mid-1870's until 1889 (when Pellegrini died and Bowles left *Vanity Fair*), "Jehu Junior," "Ape," and "Spy" were inseparable, producing a combination that made the magazine a national institution. Despite periodic rivalry between Ward and Pellegrini, "Spy" both admired and was to some extent influenced by "Ape," especially in the earlier years. Many of Ward's later drawings, however interesting, tend to lack the "bite" of the earlier ones and often are little more than photographic portraiture.

Kings, Princes, Potentates, Peers, Statesmen, Judges, Soldiers, Sailors, Artists, Authors, Actors (Fig. 66), and even a "Showman" (Fig. 62) all found their ways via the artists' pencils into the *Vanity Fair* gallery. In some cases, the *Vanity Fair* drawing may be the only pictorial record we have of a person. And even if photographs or more formal portraits are available, the caricatures and semicaricatures may still render more penetrating insights into characters, as Bowles suggested.

Generally, subjects were flattered by inclusion in the gallery, and many tried unsuccessfully to "get in." Indeed, it is interesting to speculate on why many who should have been included were not. A few were startled when seeing themselves "cartoonized," and some were outright furious. Anthony Trollope (Fig. 27), for example, could not believe that his potbelly was quite that obvious, or that he held his cigar in quite that manner. But his anger was short-lived when he recognized the fact that Ward had, as the modern "Candid Camera" says, "caught him in the act of being himself."

Other Artists

Despite their combined efforts up to 1889 and Ward's unbelievable output after that, "Spy" and "Ape" could not possibly have maintained the pace of weekly contributions without help from other contributors. The Chronological Checklist, therefore, notes numerous other signatures, along with those of Pellegrini and Ward. Artists whose signatures have been identified are:

Beerbohm, Sir Max (Max, Ruth, or Bulbo)
Braddell (KYO)
Cecioni, Andriano (did not sign, but contributed twenty-six cartoons in 1872)
Chartran, Théobald (.T., .TC.)
Dalton, F.T. (F.T.D.)
Duff, C.G. (?) (C.G.D. or Cloister)
Giles, Godfrey Douglas (G.D.G. or GD.G.)
Gleichen (?) (Glick)
Goedecker, F. (Go or FG in monogram)
Gould, Sir Francis C. (CG or FCG)
Grimm, Constantine von or de (NEMO or C. de Grimm)
L'Estrange, Roland (Ao)
Loye, Charles Auguste (MD, for pseudonym "Montbard")
Marks, A.J. (AJM)
Mellor, John Page (QUIZ or QVIZ)
Norton, Eardley (E.B.N.)
Paleologu, Jean de (PAL)
Partridge, Sir Bernard (J:B:P)

Pellegrini, Carlo (SINGE or APE)
Prosperi, Liberio (LIB)
Rees, Mrs. J.D., née Hon. Mary Dormer (MR, BINT)
Sickert, Walter Richard (SIC)
Thompson, Alfred (ATή)
Tissot, James Jacques (COÏDÉ, JTJ)
Verheyden, François (F.V.)
Vine, W. (WV in monogram)
Ward, Sir Leslie (SPY or DRAWL)
Witherby, A.G. (W.A.G. or wag)
Wright, H.C. Sepping (?) (STUFF, Stuff Gownsman, or STUFF G.)

Artists who simply signed their names include Emil Adams, Eilanley
Cock, Percy Earl, E. Flagg, Harry Furniss, Jean Baptiste Guth, Wallace
Hester, Hal Hurst, William Miller, Frank Paton, Alick P. F. Ritchie,
and S. Tel. The remaining are signatures for artists I have been unable
to identify: ALS, Ape Junior, Ast or Astor, Bede, CB, Elf, FR., GAF,
Geo. Hum, Hadge, Hay, H.C.O., Hic, Imp, Jest, K, Kite, Mouse, N.,
Nibs, Owl, Pat, Pip, Pry, Quip, Ray, Ryg, Snapp, Strickland, Sue,
Tec, VA, Vanitas, WGR, WHO, WH—, and Xit.

Those interested in further research on these artists will want to
contact London's National Portrait Gallery (London WC2H OHE,
England) for a copy of their excellent exhibition catalogue, prepared by
Richard Ormond and Eileen Harris for the 1976 exhibit of original
drawings. The booklet contains Harris' well-researched introductory
article, detailed information on the drawings in the exhibition, and a
briefly annotated listing of the artists, with sobriquets and signatures.
The Gallery owns a typescript list of artists prepared by Bowles for the
period of his editorship, 1869-1889.

The Illustrations

Although it has been difficult to select representative cartoons
from the more than two thousand in the collection, I have tried to
choose from various years, artists, and categories. Photographs for this
book were made either from prints included in the magazine itself or
collected in "Albums." The Albums contained collected cartoons for

individual years. Also, "Sets" were collected in various categories and published in response to increasing public demand. The early prints (1869–1873) measure about 7½ by 12 inches with 1- to 1½-inch white margins. Later, the size increases to 7½ by 12½ or 13 inches with slightly larger white margins. In most cases, the margins contain the caption, date, name of the lithographer, and name of the magazine. I have also included illustrations of larger prints: several "doubles" (usually about 13 by 19 inches) and one delightful "triple" (Fig. 69). Included also is one (Fig. 113) of several race horses, which appeared in 1909.

The Chronological List

For convenience, I have listed only the last names in most cases. Full names with titles may be found in the Index. Note that page numbers correspond to the years. I have indicated artists' signatures for those prints actually signed. In some cases, I have included the name in parentheses, even though the print itself was unsigned. Notes at the bottom of several pages provide further information, and those subjects illustrated in Part I are also noted.

The Subject Index

Although the Index is based on names of subjects as they actually were printed in *Vanity Fair*, I have, in several instances, inserted the given names of individuals who were listed by their titles (Bishop of, Earl of, and so on) in the magazine. My cross-listing is incomplete, but it may offer some guidance to those seeking illustrations of subjects known by both names and titles. Also, in cases where titles were later given to subjects appearing more than once, I have simply listed these separately, following names as given in *Vanity Fair*.

Since several group drawings appeared in the magazine, I have indexed a "Groups" category and have listed these chronologically by the title *Vanity Fair* gave to them. Since most of these contain numerous subjects, I have noted only principal characters in parentheses after each.

Using the Checklist

The most obvious use of this Checklist will be for those who seek a quick reference for finding if and when a particular individual was caricatured in *Vanity Fair*. It may also serve as a reference for doing further research on the magazine and its artists. For those unfamiliar with the *Vanity Fair* lithographs, the section of illustrations may serve as an introduction to this delightful series. Further information for those specifically interested in collecting the prints may be found in the *Antiques Journal* article listed in the bibliography and in the forthcoming *Collector's Guide*.

Bibliography

I have probably overlooked some information on the *Vanity Fair* cartoons that deserves inclusion here, and I will welcome learning about it. Readers may also want to consult references listed in some of the following articles, especially those by Eileen Harris. Books on caricature art, such as David Low's *British Cartoonists, Caricaturists and Comic Artists* and Werner Hoffmann's *Caricature from Leonardo to Picasso*, will also be helpful.

Harris, Eileen. "Introduction," *Vanity Fair: An Exhibition of Original Cartoons*. London: National Portrait Gallery, 1976.

———. "Carlo Pellegrini: Man and 'Ape,'" *Apollo Magazine*, January, 1976.

Mann, Ruth J. "The Unheroic Representation of Heroes," a "Historical Vignette" on several of *Vanity Fair*'s medical personalities, *Mayo Clinic Proc*, Vol 46 (March, 1971), 197–99.

Manvell, Brian. "Cartoons of Theatrical Interest Appearing in 'Vanity Fair,'" *Theatre Notebook*, Vol 19 (1965), 126–33.

Matthews, Roy. "Spy," *British History Illustrated* (June-July, 1976), 50–57.

Maunsell, H. R. "'Vanity Fair' Cartoons," a brief note identifying several artists, *Notes and Queries*, Vol 66 (April 21, 1934), 284.

Moxon, Robert K. Three short articles in the *New England Journal of Medicine* on medical personalities: Richard Owen (July 5, 1962), Sir Henry Thompson (November 1, 1962), and Erasmus Wilson (April 1, 1976).

Naylor, Leonard E. *The Irrepressible Victorian: The Story of Thomas Gibson Bowles*. London: Macdonald, 1965.

Ormond, Richard. "Catalogue," *Vanity Fair: An Exhibition of Original Cartoons*. London: National Portrait Gallery, 1976.

Savory, Jerold. "Collecting *Vanity Fair* Caricatures," *The Antiques Journal* (March, 1978).

————. Short notes on individual prints in: *The Arnoldian* (Fall, 1978), *Notes and Queries* (forthcoming, 1978), *Studies in Browning* (Fall, 1977), and *Oceans* (November-December, 1977).

———— "Well-Known 'Vanities,' " *American History Illustrated* (January, 1978).

Vanity Fair: A Weekly Show of Political, Social, and Literary Wares (November, 1868–February, 1914). Several collections are available in America and England. One nearly complete collection with all but a few cartoons still intact is in the Free Library of Philadelphia.

Ward, Mrs. E. M. *Memories of Ninety Years*. Second Edition. New York: H. Holt and Company, 1925.

Ward, Leslie. *Forty Years of "Spy."* London: Chatto & Windus, 1915 (reissued by Singing Tree Press, Book Tower, Detroit, 1969).

PART I

ILLUSTRATIONS FROM *VANITY FAIR*

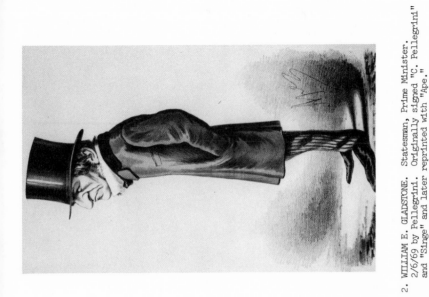

1. BENJAMIN DISRAELI. Statesman, Author, Prime Minister. 1/30/69 by Pellegrini. The first cartoon in *Vanity Fair*. Originally signed "Singe," it appeared later with "Ape's" familiar signature.

2. WILLIAM E. GLADSTONE. Statesman, Prime Minister. 2/6/69 by Pellegrini. Originally signed "C. Pellegrini" and "Singe" and later reprinted with "Ape."

3

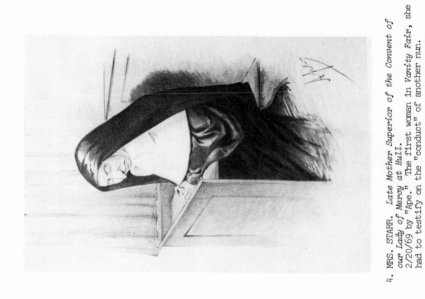

4. MRS. STARR. *Late Mother Superior of the Convent of our Lady of Mercy at Hull.* 2/20/69 by "Ape." The first woman in *Vanity Fair*, she had to testify on the "conduct" of another nun.

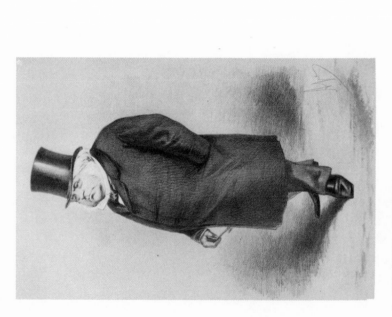

3. JOHN BRIGHT. Statesman. 2/13/69 by "Ape." The first cartoon to appear with Pellegrini's familiar signature.

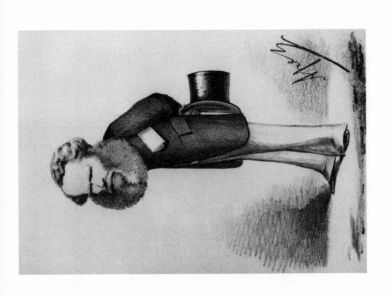

6. M. E. GRANT-DUFF. Politician and Parliamentarian, Author. 10/2/69 by "Ape." Labelled a "philosophic liberal," this is a good early example of the "ape-like" cast in Pellegrini's work.

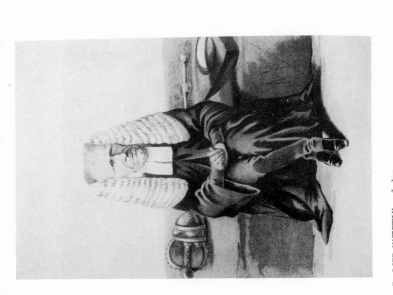

5. LORD HATHERLY. Judge. 3/20/69 by "Ape." This is the first of many colorful cartoons of legal figures to appear during the magazine's history.

8. POPE PIUS IX.
   1/1/70, Unsigned. The first of several Popes to appear
   in the magazine.

7. PENZANCE (JAMES WILDE). Judge.
   12/18/69, Unsigned, but by Pellegrini.

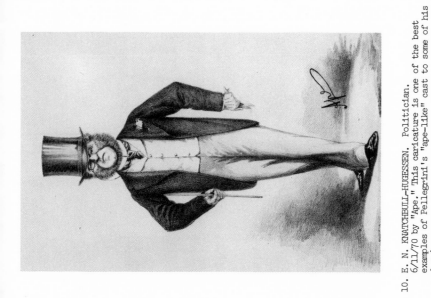

9. HENRI ROCHEFORT. French "journalist, lanternier, and demagogue." 1/22/70, Unsigned. Severely attacked by *Vanity Fair*, the cartoon reflects "Jehu, Jr.'s" commentary.

10. E. N. KNATCHBULL-HUGESSEN. Politician. 6/11/70 by "Ape." This caricature is one of the best examples of Pellegrini's "ape-like" cast to some of his drawings.

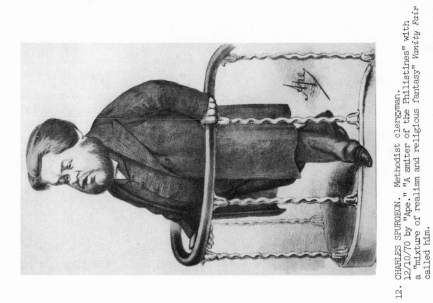

12. CHARLES SPURGEON. Methodist clergyman. 12/10/70 by "Ape." "A smiter of the Philistines" with a "mixture of realism and religious fantasy" *Vanity Fair* called him.

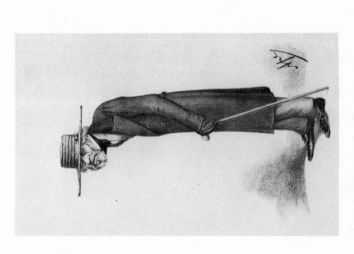

11. THOMAS CARLYLE. Major Victorian writer-philosopher. 10/22/70 by "Ape." Carlyle is described as "the Diogenes of the Modern Corinthians without his tub."

8

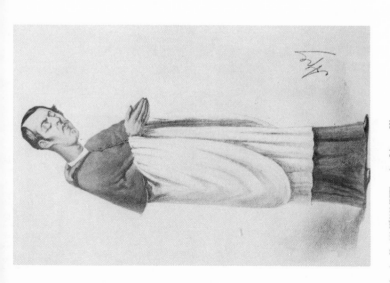

13. A. H. MACKONOCHIE. Anglican Vicar.
12/31/70 by "Ape." "He makes
religion a tragedy and the movements of his muscles
a solemn ceremony. He is the antithesis of
Mr. Spurgeon."

14. THOMAS HUXLEY. Scientist and writer.
1/28/71 by "Ape." The "inventor of protoplasm" and
advocate of women's education, said the magazine.

15. ALFRED TENNYSON. Poet Laureate.
7/22/71 by "Ape." *Vanity Fair* comments on a current
"fashion to doubt his genius and to depreciate his
works."

16. CHARLES DARWIN. Naturalist, Author.
9/30/71, Unsigned. The author of *Origin of Species* is
shown in a characteristic posture in a favorite chair.

18. DR. FREDERICK QUIN. Physician and scientist.
1/20/72, Unsigned. A delightful caricature of the
founder of the British Homeopathic Society.

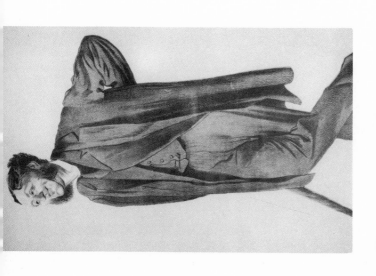

17. MATTHEW ARNOLD. Major Victorian poet, essayist, and
critic.
4/11/71, Unsigned. "I say, the critic must keep out
of the region of immediate practice."

11

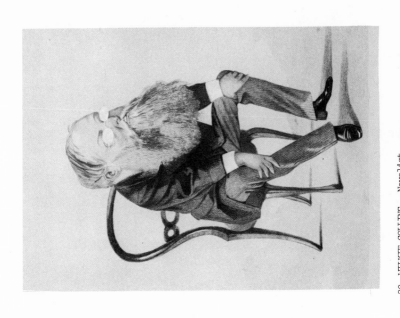

20. WILKIE COLLINS. Novelist.
2/3/72, Unsigned (by Cecioni). "He is entitled to be
called the novelist who invented Sensation."

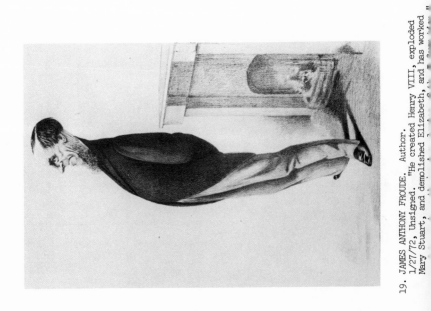

19. JAMES ANTHONY FROUDE. Author.
1/27/72, Unsigned. "He created Henry VIII, exploded
Mary Stuart, and demolished Elizabeth, and has worked

21. JOHN RUSKIN. Poet and Essayist. "An incurable poet and artist in a materialistic and money-grubbing generation." 2/17/72, Unsigned (by Cecioni).

22. ULYSSES S. GRANT. American President. 6/1/72, Unsigned. Despite his British reputation for being "dull," *Vanity Fair* presents Grant favorably, both in words and picture.

13

23. HORACE GREELEY. American newspaperman and politician. 7/20/72, Unsigned. Grant's opposing candidate in the 1872 election is hit with bitter satire, both visually and verbally, by *Vanity Fair*.

24. NEWMAN HALL. Congregational minister. 11/23/72, Unsigned. Although *Vanity Fair*'s commentary is not especially hard-hitting, the cartoon suggests a "satanic" bearing.

26. JOHN STUART MILL. Author-Philosopher.
3/24/73 by "Spy." The second to bear the famous "Spy"
signature, this is a good caricature of the Utilitarian
philosopher.

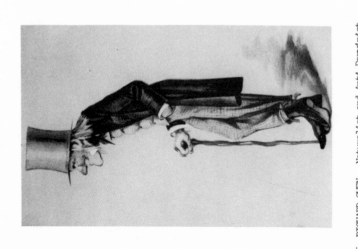

25. RICHARD OWEN. Naturalist and Anti-Darwinist.
3/1/73. Unsigned, but this cartoon was Leslie Ward's
first contribution to the magazine.

27. ANTHONY TROLLOPE. Novelist.
4/5/73 by "Spy." The caricature drew some short-lived
anger from the well-known novelist of the day.

28. E. M. WARD. Artist of the Royal Academy.
12/20/73 by "Spy." A realistically "portly," but
obviously admiring, semicaricature of "Spy's" respected
father.

30. ALGERNON CHARLES SWINBURNE. Poet.
11/21/74 by "Ape." The poet is shown here shortly after
his publication of *Songs Before Sunrise*.

29. ARTHUR SULLIVAN. Musician.
3/14/74 by "Ape." Here, with his eyeglass and baton,
is the "other half" of the Gilbert and Sullivan
operetta duo.

31. JOHN W. COLENSO. Clergyman and Bishop of Natal.
11/28/74 by "Ape." Colenso made his "mark" with a
Zulu-inspired book questioning Biblical literalism.

32. HENRY IRVING. Actor.
12/19/74 by "Ape." Irving was one of the best-known
Victorian "mannerist" actors.

18

33. DWIGHT L. MOODY. Evangelist.
4/3/75 by "Ape." "Full of Yankee humor and unexpected point," Moody appealed to "emotional and sentimental aspects of the Faith."

34. IRA D. SANKEY. Gospel-singer.
4/10/75 by "Ape." As D.L. Moody's musical sidekick, Sankey's "singing is as vulgar as Mr. Moody's preaching," said *Vanity Fair*.

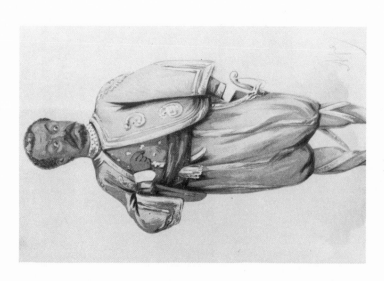

35. SIGNOR TOMMASO SALVINI. Actor. 5/22/75 by "Ape." Founder of the Italian Dramatic Society, he is shown in his role as "Othello."

36. ROBERT BROWNING. Poet. 11/20/75 by "Ape." "The best of our professors of modern poetry," he is depicted here at age 63, at the publica-

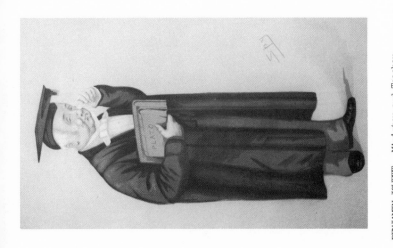

38. BENJAMIN JOWETT. Minister and Teacher.
2/26/76 by "Spy." His fame coming from *Essays and Reviews*, he "bears a resemblance to the conventional cherub of the tombstone."

37. CHARLES OLD GOODFORD. Clergyman.
1/22/76 by "Spy." *Old Goody* is depicted by Ward as an almost Dickensian character with his top hat and umbrella.

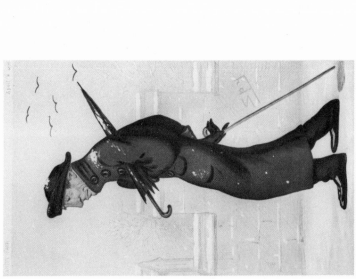

39. GERALD V. WELLESLEY. Clergyman. 4/18/76 by "Spy." *The Old Dean* is shown making his way through a snowstorm.

40. JOHN HENRY NEWMAN. Catholic Cardinal, poet, essayist. 1/20/77 by "Spy." Oxford Movement leader, he turned from Anglicanism to the Church of Rome where he continued to

41. ARTHUR TOOTH. High Church clergyman.
    2/10/77 by "Spy." Tooth was imprisoned for his
    "revival of Popish practices," thus becoming the
    Protomartyr of Ritual.

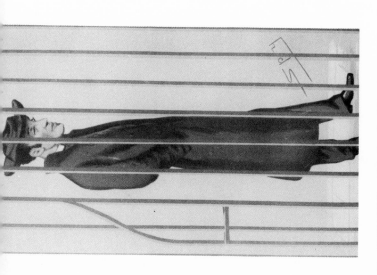

42. RICHARD WAGNER. Composer.
    5/9/77 by "Spy." This lively cartoon of the composer—
    conductor is captioned *The Music of the Future.*

44. GIUSEPPE GARIBALDI. Italian patriot.
7/15/78 by "T." This semicaricature of the famous
General was one of Chartran's first contributions.

43. JAMES WHISTLER. Artist. 1/2/78 by "Spy." One of Ward's best character portraits.

46. SARAH BERNHARDT. Actress.
7/5/79 by "T." One of two drawings of the famous actress in the series.

45. DISRAELI. Politician and Prime Minister.
7/20/78 by "Ape." Another portrait of Beaconsfield, a popular subject with *Vanity Fair* artists.

47. "THE TREASURY BENCH."
7/6/80 by "T." This drawing, done on a horizontal format, shows Gladstone, Hartington, and Chamberlain in characteristic poses.

48. FRANCIS E.C. BYNG. Clergyman. "A perfect study for the caricaturist," wrote Leslie Ward of Byng.
10/18/79 by "Spy."

49. "FORCE NO REMEDY."
12/7/81 by Harry Furniss. This is an unusual drawing,
showing Parnell as a political prisoner.

50. "HER MAJESTY'S OPPOSITION."
7/5/81 by "T." Captioned *Birth, Behavior, and Business,* the group consists of Northcote, Manner, and Cross.

52. OSCAR WILDE. Irish poet, dramatist, and novelist. 5/24/84 by "Ape." An excellent character portrait of the well-known wit.

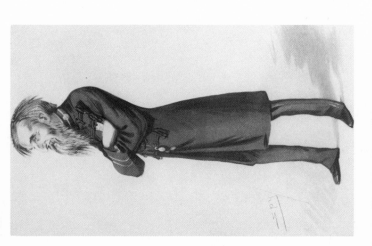

51. "GENERAL" BOOTH. Evangelist. 11/25/82 by "Spy." This general, of course, is non-military. He is the founder of the Salvation Army.

54. FIELD MARSHAL COUNT VON MOLTKE.
8/23/84 by "Go." This cartoon of the military leader
is a good example of Goedecker's comic touch.

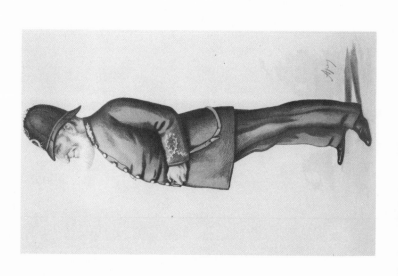

53. POLICE-INSPECTOR E. DENNING.
8/6/84 by "Ape." A good example of a British "Bobby"
in full dress.

56. M. LOUIS PASTEUR. French chemist. 1/8/87 by "T." A delightful drawing of the founder of modern bacteriology and immunology.

55. OLIVER WENDELL HOLMES. Physician, poet, essayist. 6/19/86 by "Spy." One of a number of Americans in *Vanity Fair*. Dr. Holmes deserves to be included for his eyebrows alone!

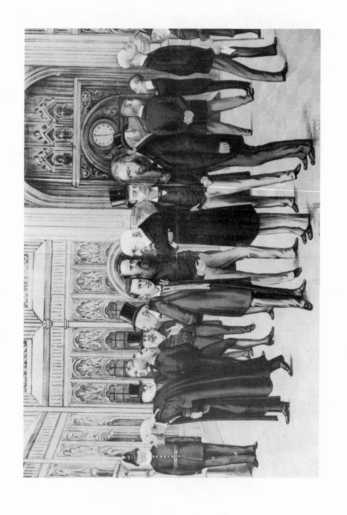

57. "LOBBY OF HOUSE OF COMMONS."
12/25/86 by "Lib." One of several double-sized prints showing prominent
political leaders of the day. Here are Bright, Harcourt, Chamberlain, Parnell,
and Gladstone, along with others.

58. JAMES L. JOYNES. Clergyman and Educator.
7/16/87 by "Spy." A true caricature, showing Joynes
in academic clothes, complete with switch.

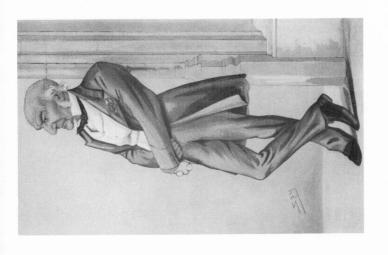

59. W. E. GLADSTONE. Prime Minister.
11/5/87 by "Spy." A later portrait of *The Grand Old*
Man.

61. THOMAS GIBSON BOWLES. Writer, editor, and politician. 7/13/89 by "Spy." One of two drawings of "Tommy" Bowles in *Vanity Fair*, the magazine he founded. He retired from the editorship in this year.

60. CARLO PELLEGRINI. Artist and "Ape." 4/27/89 by "A.J.M." (A.J. Marks). This drawing appeared the year of Pellegrini's death as a memorial to the presiding genius of the magazine's caricature lithographs.

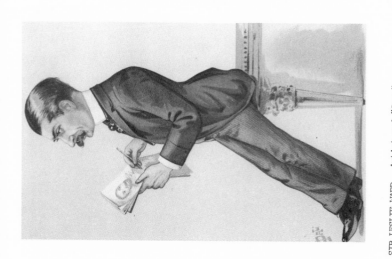

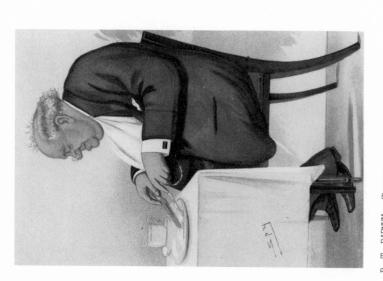

62. P. T. BARNUM. Showman.
11/16/89 by "Spy." The American showman, popular in
England, is shown at one of his favorite pastimes.

63. SIR LESLIE WARD. Artist and "Spy."
11/23/89 by "Pal" (Jean de Paleologu). Ward was by far
the magazine's most prolific contributor and the main
cartoonist after Pellegrini's death.

64. ALDERMAN SAVORY. Lord Mayor of London. 11/1/90 by "Spy." (Editor's note: I include this drawing for obvious reasons! Actually, there _is_ some resemblance!)

65. HERBERT H. ASQUITH. Parliamentarian and Prime Minister. 8/1/91 by "Spy." Asquith was a favorite subject for _Vanity Fair_ artists.

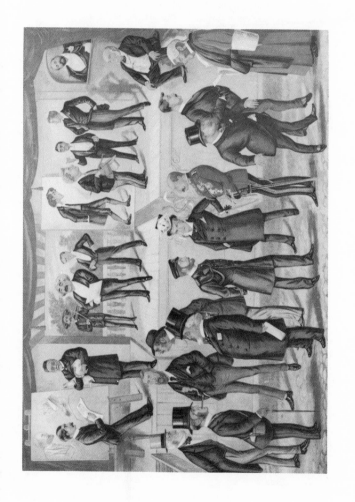

66. "IN VANITY FAIR."
11/29/90 by "Spy" and others. This double print is a striking composite of 22
of *Vanity Fair*'s most popular subjects, including "Spy" in the upper left.
Note also the sketches on the easel.

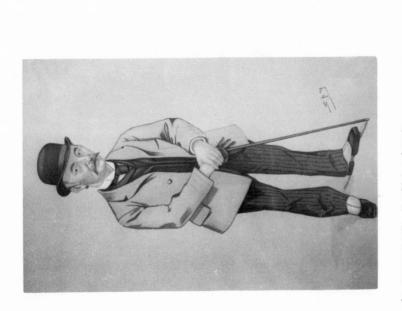

67. THOMAS HARDY. Novelist and poet.
6/4/92 by "Spy." This drawing of the popular writer
was in response to the popularity of his novel *Tess
of the D'Urbervilles*.

68. H. COZENS-HARDY. Judge. Cozens-Hardy appeared several times
4/13/93 by "Spy." in the magazine, but this is by far the finest of the
drawings.

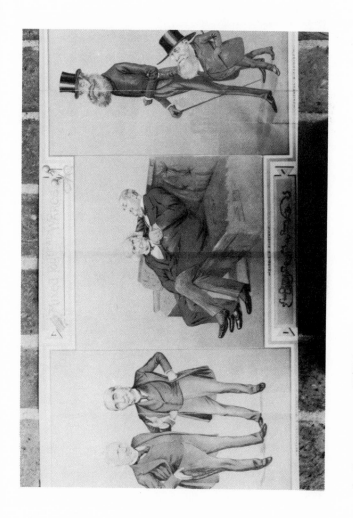

69. "MIXED POLITICAL WARES."
12/3/92 by "Spy." This one is unique as the only triple-sized lithograph of the more than 2,000 published. Here, with assigned "labels," are: Gladstone ("Babble"), Harcourt ("Bluster"), Spencer ("Faithful"), Ripon ("Padist"), Campbell-Bannerman ("Methodical"), and Fowler ("Methodist").

71. HERR EDUARD STRAUSS. Musician.
8/29/95 by "E.B.N." A striking portrait of an
imposing figure, by Eardley Norton.

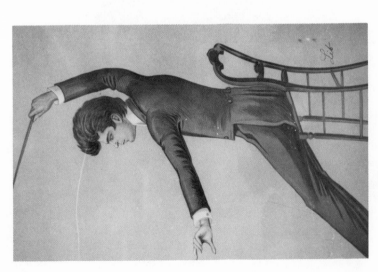

70. SIGNOR PIETRO MASCAGNI. Musician.
8/24/93 by "Lib." This drawing by Liberio Prosperi
shows Mascagni conducting "Cavalleria Rusticana."

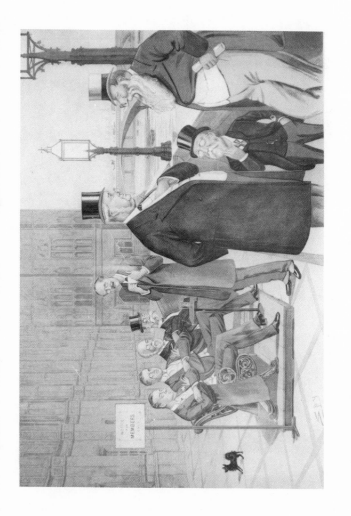

72. "ON THE TERRACE."
11/30/93 by "Spy." This beautiful double print with Balfour, Chamberlain, Harcourt, and others shows the Terrace of Parliament with the Thames in the background. Note also the dog!

41

73. "AT COWES." "Spy." Another double print, of distinguished yachtsmen, dominated 12/6/94 by the central figure, H.R.H., The Prince of Wales.

74. MR. CAIRD, MASTER OF BALLIOL.
4/4/95 by "Spy." One of the more interesting character portraits of the many scholars in the series.

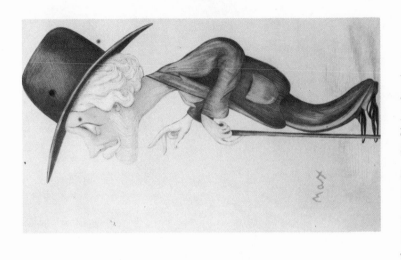

75. ALFRED AUSTIN. Poet Laureate.
2/20/96 by "Spy." A poet of questionable genius,
Austin is described by Ward: "His dress was that of
a country squire and not that of a long-haired
poet."

76. GEORGE MEREDITH. Novelist and poet.
9/24/96 by "Max." This delightful caricature of Meredith
is a good example of Max Beerbohm's talent as a caricaturist.

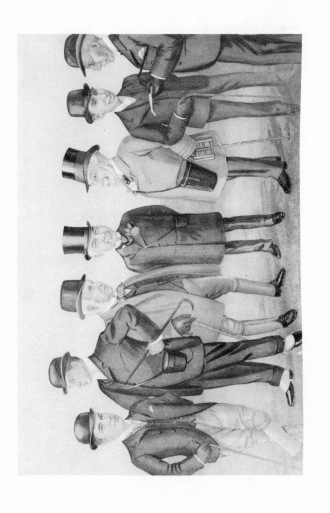

77. "ON THE HEATH." English pride in thoroughbreds and the turf is evident 11/26/96 by "Spy." Here, John Porter and other Derby-winning trainers throughout the series. are seen with distinguished turf enthusiasts.

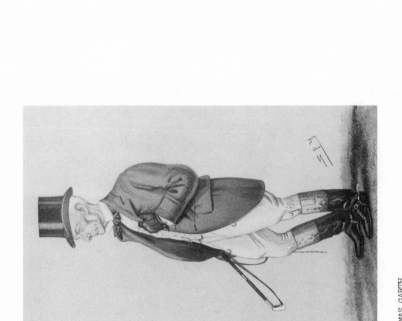

78. THOMAS GARTH.
10/29/96 by "Spy." One of many red-coated fox-
hunters in the *Vanity Fair* series, this one is cap-

79. MAX BEERBOHM. Artist.
12/9/97 by "Sic." One of three cartoons contributed by
W. R. Sickert, this one is of a fellow-caricaturist
who signed "Max," "Ruth," or "Bulbo."

46

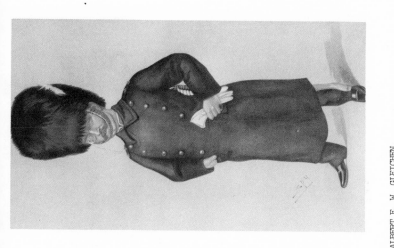

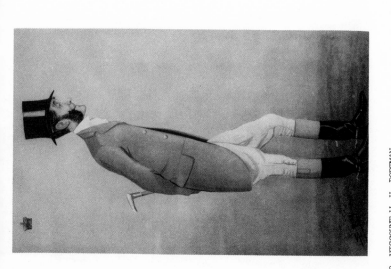

80. VISCOUNT W. H. PORTMAN.
11/3/98 by "Spy." Another "red-coat." Many of the *Vanity Fair* cartoons are best appreciated only when seen in their full color. This is one.

81. ALBERT E. W. GLEICHEN.
11/13/98 by "Spy." This is a good example of the variety of military regalia found in the *Vanity Fair* drawings.

47

83. CARL MUCK. Musician. Striking in its light and dark
    contrasts, this is by the clever caricaturist
    7/27/99 by "W.A.G." Striking in its light and dark
    A. G. Witherby.

82. SIR WILLIAM V. HARCOURT. This drawing by C. G. Duff (?)
    5/11/99 by "Cloister." This drawing by C. G. Duff (?)
    shows the Chancellor of Exchequer in a striking but
    unheroic attitude.

48

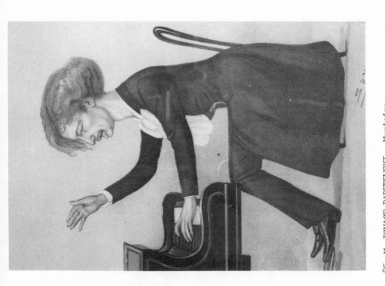

85. M. IGNACE PADEREWSKI. Musician. 12/28/99 by "Spy." An interesting cartoon of the famous pianist.

84. THE COMTE DE DION. This drawing by the French painter Jean Baptiste Guth 10/12/99 by "Guth." is one of the few in the series of "automobiles."

86. "AT RENNES." "Guth." This double-sized print is the trial scene of Captain Dreyfus (standing, in center).

87. BAHADUR, MAHARAJA OF PATIALA.
1/4/1900 by "M.R." One of several of foreign royalty,
this unusual cartoon shows the Maharaja as a polo
player.

88. FIELD-MARSHAL LORD ROBERTS.
6/21/1900 by "Spy." Ward writes: "This cartoon, on
account of the subject, beat the record for popularity, and its sale exceeded that of all other cartoons
in *Vanity Fair*."

89. JOHN D. P. FRENCH. Cavalry Leader. 7/12/1900 by "G.D.G." General French is done here by Godfrey Douglas Gile, a painter who was also a soldier.

90. WINSTON CHURCHILL. Statesman; Later, Prime Minister. 9/27/1900 by "Spy." The young Winston is shown in characteristic stance.

91. QUEEN VICTORIA.
1/31/1901 by "Guth." The only *Vanity Fair* lithograph of the long-reigning Queen, this is a black-and-white memorial re-print of an 1897 drawing. Victoria died in 1901.

92. LYOF M. TOLSTOI. Author
10/24/1901 by "Snapp." The contributor of two cartoons, those of Ibsen (#94) and this one of the famed Russian novelist of *War and Peace*, Snapp's style was unique.

93. M. SANTOS DUMONT. 11/14/1901 by "Geo. Hum." A few of the cartoons reflect the on-coming 20th century revolution in auto and air travel. "Geo. Hum." is unknown to the authors. Many of the [...]

94. HENRIK IBSEN, Playwright. 12/12/1901 by "Snapp." One of two by Snapp (see Tolstoi, #92), this one captures the stunning white "mane" of the subject of "Hedda Gabler" and other plays [...]

95. "KIRBY GATE." "C.B." Mrs. Asquith and other male and female fox-hunters are colorfully captured in this delightful double.

96. EDWARD VII. "Spy." A good portrait of the recently crowned regent of the new "Edwardian Era."
6/19/1902 by "Spy."

97. F. S. JACKSON. Sportsman. One of a number of cricketeers, rugby players, and other athletes in the collection.
8/28/1902 by "Spy."

98. THEODORE ROOSEVELT. American President. 9/4/1902 by "Flagg." Perhaps as well-known as any of the magazine's cartoons, this one of "Teddy" has been reprinted several times.

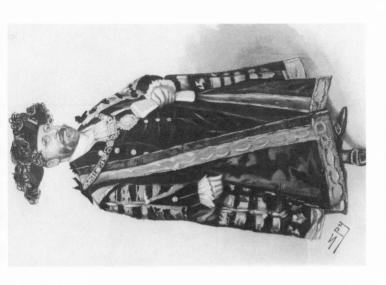

99. SIR JOSEPH C. DIMSDALE. Lord Mayor. 10/23/1902 by "Spy." This one of the "New Lord Mayor" is especially attractive because of the regalia.

100. "HEADS OF LAW." The legal lithographs have continued to be among the most popular. 11/28/1902 by "Spy." Here is an excellent double with Chief Justice Alverstone and colleagues.

102. R. J. CAMPBELL, Minister. 1/24/1904 by "Spy." One of Ward's most colorful drawings, for which he made numerous preliminary sketches. Pulpit action is captured in the cartoon labelled *Fearless But Intemperate*.

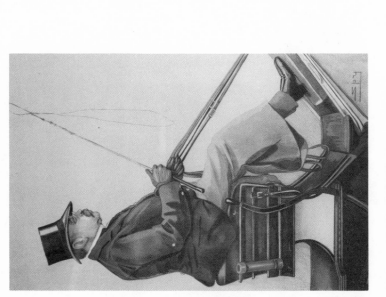

101. BARON ADOLPH WILHELM DEICHMANN. 5/14/1903 by "Spy." Looking as if he had been driving for a straight 24 hours, Deichman is shown with "four-in-hand."

104. SIR HIRAM STEVENS MAXIM. Inventor. 12/15/1904 by "Spy." Born in Maine (U.S.A.), he invented a tricycle, mousetrap, blackboard, and the famous Maxim gun. His "latest" is in the background.

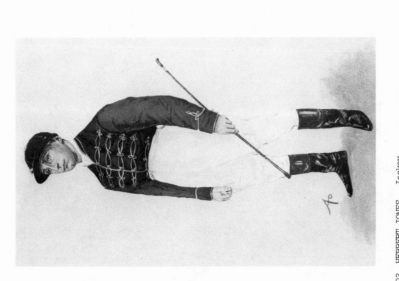

103. HERBERT JONES. Jockey. 9/29/1904 by "Ao." This portrait by Roland L'Estrange is one of several jockeys in the series.

105. AUGUSTE RODIN. Sculptor.
12/29/1904 by "Imp." Captioned *He Thinks in Marble*,
the drawing suggests the French artist's resemblance
to his own work!

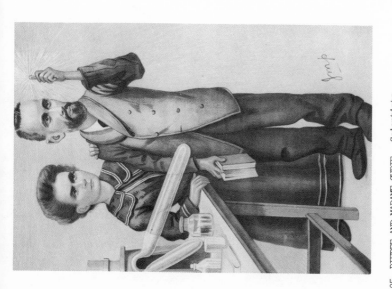

105. PIERRE AND MADAME CURIE. Scientists.
12/22/1904 by "Imp." The discoverers of radium are
captured in the dramatic moment.

61

107. SIR EDWIN RAY LANKESTER. Scientist.
1/12/1905 by "Spy." Founder of the Plymouth Marine
Lab, Professor Lankester is shown with some favorite
"winged and finny freaks."

108. H. W. LUCY. Parliamentarian.
8/31/1905 by "Spy." The largest group of *Vanity Fair*
cartoons is the politicians, both known and unknown
today. Here is one of the better drawings of an "M.P."

110. GEORGE BERNARD SHAW. Dramatist and Playwright. 12/28/1905 by "Ruth." This Beerbohm cartoon of "G.B.S." is one of Max's finest.

109. THOMAS GIBSON BOWLES. Parliamentarian and Journalist. 10/19/1905 by "Spy." Done 16 years after Bowles left *Vanity Fair*, this one shows "Jehu Junior" as a Member of Parliament.

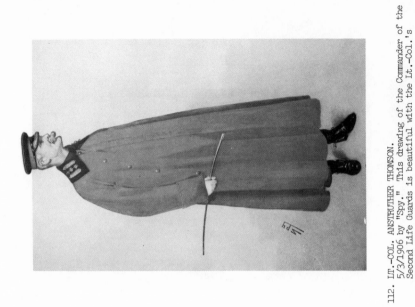

112. LT.-COL. ANSTRUTHER THOMSON.
5/3/1906 by "Spy." This drawing of the Commander of the
Second Life Guards is beautiful with the Lt.-Col.'s
bright red coat.

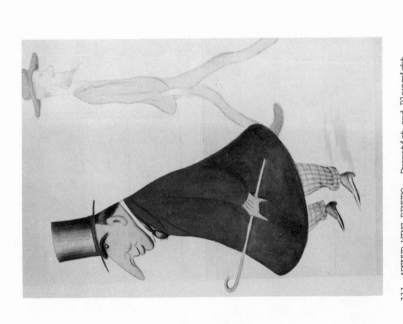

111. ARTHUR WING PINERO. Dramatist and Playwright.
2/1/1906 by "Bulbo." Another Beerbohm under a
different sobriquet, this one of Pinero shows Shaw
in the background.

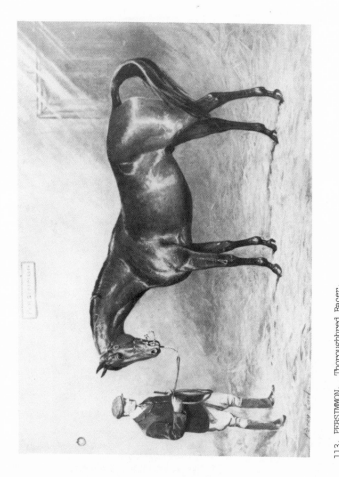

113. PERSIMMON. Thoroughbred Racer. Hardly a "caricature," this is one of a dozen
11/24/1909 by "Percy Earl." famous race horses appearing in 1909 issues of *Vanity Fair*. Earl did most.

115. WOODROW WILSON. American President. 3/12/1913 by "W. Hester." One of the later lithographs in the magazine, this portrait stands in marked contrast to the caricature art of earlier cartoonists.

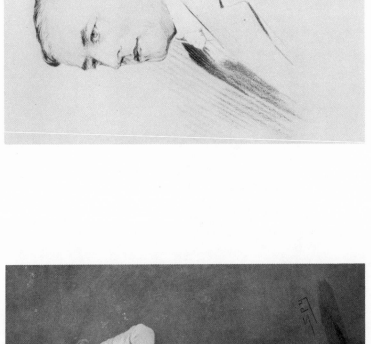

114. SAMUEL CLEMENS. Author-humorist. 5/13/1903 by "Spy." Leslie Ward's account of his effort to "capture" his beloved subject with white suit and calabash pipe is an amusing story about *Mark Twain*.

PART II

CHRONOLOGICAL CHECKLIST

Date	Subject	Signed	Date	Subject	Signed
1/30	DISRAELI *1	Singe	7/3	PETERSBOROUGH	Ape
		(Later, Ape)	7/10	SALISBURY	Ape
			7/17	KIMBERLEY	Ape
2/6	GLADSTONE *2	Singe	7/24	OXFORD	Ape
		(Later, Ape)	7/31	CAIRNS	Ape
2/13	BRIGHT *3	Ape			
2/20	STARR *4	Ape	8/7	SOMERSET	Ape
2/27	LOWE	Ape	8/14	FORTESQUE	Ape
			8/21	BRUCE	Ape
3/6	FORSTER	Ape	8/28	LAYARD	Ape
3/13	GRANVILLE	Ape			
3/20	HATHERLY *5	Ape	9/4	NAPOLEON III	Coidé
3/27	HARTINGTON	Ape	9/11	CARNARVON	Ape
			9/18	ISABELLA II	Coidé
4/3	CARDWELL	Ape	9/25	ABERCORN	Ape
4/10	STANSFELD	Ape			
4/17	ARGYLL	Ape	10/2	GRANT-DUFF *6	Ape
4/24	CLARENDON	Ape	10/9	LEOPOLD II	Coidé
			10/16	ALEXANDER II	Coidé
5/1	SYDNEY	Ape	10/23	AYRTON	Ape
5/8	GREY	Ape	10/30	ABDUL-AZIZ	Coidé
5/15	WESTBURY	Ape			
5/22	GREY and RIPON	Ape	11/6	TEMPLE	
5/29	DERBY	Ape	11/13	SHAFTESBURY	Ape
			11/20	MANNERS	Ape
6/5	RUSSELL	Ape	11/27	LESSEPS	
6/12	GOSCHEN	Ape			
		(Reversed)	12/4	ZETLAND	
6/19	CHILDERS	Ape	12/11	COCKBURN	Ape
6/26	STANLEY	Ape	12/18	PENZANCE *7	(Pellegrini)
			12/25	TAIT (CANTERBURY)	Coidé

*Indicates subject is illustrated in Part I.
NOTE: Unsigned cartoons this year were by Tissot or Pellegrini.

Date	Subject	Signed	Date	Subject	Signed
1/1	PIUS IX *8		7/2	SPENCER	Ape
1/8	BOVILL	Ape	7/9	SUTHERLAND	Ape
1/15	OLLIVIER		7/16	WESTMINSTER	
1/22	ROCHEFORT *9		7/23	ELCHO	Ape
1/29	VICTOR EMMANUEL I		7/30	GORDON-LENNOX	Ape
2/5	CHELMSFORD		8/6	HALIFAX (WOOD)	Ape
2/12	PAKINGTON		8/13	NEWDEGATE	Ape
2/19	COLLIER	Atn	8/20	STRATHNAIRN	Ape
2/26	TOWNSHEND	(Thompson)	8/27	BULWER	Ape
3/5	BALLENTINE		9/3	HOUGHTON	Ape
3/12	DENISON	Atn	9/10	BERESFORD-HOPE	Ape
3/19	PEEL	Atn	9/17	TROCHU	
3/26	RICHMOND	Atn	9/24	PRINCE FRED. WM.	
4/2	POLLOCK	Atn	10/1	MONTAGU	Ape
4/9	DUFFERIN	Atn	10/8	NORTHCOTE	Ape
4/16	NAWAB NAZIM	Atn	10/15	VON BISMARCK-SCHOENAUSEN	
4/23	CAMBRIDGE	Atn	10/22	CARLYLE *11	Ape
4/30	COLERIDGE	(Pellegrini)	10/29	LYTTON	Ape
5/7	ROUS	Atn	11/5	VIVIAN	Ape
5/14	PRINCE TECK	Atn	11/12	BISH. LONDON	
5/21	HAWLEY	Atn		(JACKSON)	Ape
5/28	OSBORNE	Atn	11/19	LORN	Ape
			11/26	MURCHISON	Ape
6/4	VERNON-HARCOURT	Atn			
6/11	KNATCHBULL-HUGESSEN		12/3	BRUNNOW	Ape
	*10	Ape	12/10	SPURGEON *12	Ape
6/18	DUDLEY	Ape	12/17	FERGUSSON	Ape
6/26	RANELAGH	Ape	12/24	STORKS	Ape
			12/31	MACKONOCHIE *13	Ape

*Indicates subject is illustrated in Part I.
NOTE: Unsigned cartoons are likely by either Thompson or Pellegrini.

Date	Subject	Signed	Date	Subject	Signed
1/7	KING OF PRUSSIA	Coidé	7/1	SHAW-LEFEVRE	Ape
1/14	APPONYI	Ape	7/8	MARLBOROUGH	Ape
1/21	LAWRENCE	Ape	7/15	SKELMERSDALE	Ape
1/28	HUSLEY *14	Ape	7/22	TENNYSON *15	Ape
			7/29	MIALL	Ape
2/4	PASHA	Ape			
2/11	MONSELL	Ape	8/5	BENTWICK	
2/18	WHALLEY	Ape	8/12	LOCKE	
2/25	MANNING	Ape	8/19	COLE	
			8/26	RANCES Y VILLANEUVA	
3/4	CADORNA	Ape			
3/11	HUNT	Ape	9/2	SALDANHA	
3/18	NOEL	Ape	9/9	GURNEY	
3/25	DOWSE	Ape	9/16	RUTLAND	
			9/23	WHYTE-NELVILLE	
4/1	LYTTELTON	Ape	9/39	DARWIN *16	
4/8	HARROWBY	Ape			
4/15	EBURY	Ape	10/7	LUSK	
4/22	NORMANBY	Ape	10/14	EATON	
4/29	GRANT	Ape	10/21	VOYSEY	
			10/28	PENDER	(Tissot)
5/6	MAY	Ape			
5/13	MILLAIS	Ape	11/4	KELLY	
5/20	BASS	Ape	11/11	ARNOLD *17	
5/27	ROTHSCHILD	Ape	11/18	DAWSON-DAMER	
			11/25	DILKE	
6/3	SHAW	Ape			
6/10	TICHBORNE	Ape	12/2	COCHRANE	
6/17	BORTHWICK	Ape	12/9	MUNDELLA	
6/24	ARCHBSHP. YORK	Ape	12/16	DODSON	
			12/23	DAVENDISH-BENTICK	
			12/30	GREGORY	

*Indicates subject is illustrated in Part I.
NOTE: Unsigned cartoons this year are by either Tissot or Pellegrini.

Date	Subject	Signed	Date	Subject	Signed
1/6	THIERS		7/6	COSTA	
1/13	CORK and ORRERY		7/13	LEEMAN	
1/20	QUIN *18		7/20	GREELEY *23	(Nast)
1/27	FROUDE *19		7/27	BOUVERIE	
2/3	COLLINS *20	(Cecioni)	8/3	DELAHUNTY	
2/10	WALPOLE	(Cecioni)	8/10	HORSMAN	
2/17	RUSKIN *21	(Cecioni)	8/17	RADSTOCK	(Cecioni)
2/24	GLYN		8/24	VAUGHAN	
			8/31	VILLIERS	
3/2	KINGLAKE				
3/9	SMITH		9/7	CAPEL	
3/16	PALMER		9/14	ENFIELD	
3/23	MAGUIRE		9/21	A.P. STANLEY	
3/30	KINGSLEY	(Cecioni)	9/28	O'LOGHLEN	(Cecioni)
4/6	TYNDALL		10/5	ADAMS	
4/13	CUMMING		10/12	BINNEY	(MD; Loye)
4/20	HARDY		10/19	GAMBETTA	
4/27	DIXON		10/26	COWEN	
5/4	AMADEUS (SPAIN)		11/2	H.M. STANLEY	
5/11	LAWSON	(Nast)	11/9	WATERLOW	
5/18	FISH		11/16	BRAND	
5/25	SUMNER		11/23	HALL *24	
			11/30	EYKYN	
6/1	GRANT *22				
6/8	HUGHES		12/7	GOLDSMID	
6/15	MORLEY		12/14	REUTER	(Delfico)
6/22	WELLINGTON		12/21	FAWCETT	
6/29	LEIGHTON		12/28	GOLDNEY	

*Indicates subject is illustrated in Part I.
NOTE: Unsigned cartoons this year were contributed by Cecioni (26), Delfico, Loye (7). The American artist Thomas Nast did five this year, including the one of Horace Greeley.

Date	Subject	Signed	Date	Subject	Signed
1/4	ST. ALBANS		7/5	NASSER (PERSIA)	Spy
1/11	CRAWFORD		7/12	RAWLINSON	Spy
1/18	GILPIN		7/19	AIREY	Spy
1/25	BUCCLEUCH		7/26	COLVILLE	Spy
2/1	GALLOWAY		8/2	TREVELYAN	
2/8	BACON		8/9	FITZGERALD	Spy
2/15	SAMUDA		8/16	LAING	Spy
2/22	KARSLAKE		8/23	WILTON	
			8/30	GOMM	Spy
3/1	OWEN *25	(Ward)			
3/8	REID		9/6	COLLINS	Spy
3/15	PLIMSOLL	(WV; W.Vine)	9/13	COLONSAY	Spy
3/22	LEVY	Spy	9/20	FRERE	Spy
3/29	MILL *26	Spy	9/27	BENEDICT	Spy
4/5	TROLLOPE *27	Spy	10/4	CAMPBELL and	
4/12	RUSSELL			STRATHEDEN	Spy
4/19	HEADLAM	Spy	10/11	CLIFFORD	Spy
4/26	JENNER	Spy	10/18	HAMILTON-DOUGLAS	
			10/25	HARRINGTON	
5/3	BUTT	Spy			
5/10	FRITH	Spy	11/1	KENEALY	Spy
5/17	LAIRD	Spy	11/8	PRINCE OF WALES	
5/24	MELLOR	Spy	11/15	HOGG	Spy
5/31	LUSH	Spy	11/22	BATHURST	
			11/29	WALLACE	Spy
6/7	DAGLISH	Spy			
6/14	WILLIAMS-WYNN	Spy	12/6	DORAN	Spy
6/21	HAWKINS	Spy	12/13	PARRY	Spy
6/28	HIBBERT		12/20	WARD, E.M. *28	Spy
			12/27	DOYLE	

*Indicates subject is illustrated in Part I.
  NOTE: Unsigned cartoons this year were contributed by Delfico,
       Epinay, Lyall, and Vine.

Date	Subject	Signed	Date	Subject	Signed
1/3	LUMLEY	Ape	7/4	TAYLOR	Ape
1/10	EDINBURGH	Ape	7/11	BEDFORD	Ape
1/17	PANIZZI	Ape	7/18	PRAED	Ape
1/24	WOMBWELL	Ape	7/25	HARRIS	Ape
1/31	DESART	Ape			
			8/1	THOMPSON	Ape
2/7	CARRINGTON	Ape	8/8	SCLATER-BOOTH	Ape
2/14	JOHNSTONE	Ape	8/15	HELPS	Ape
2/21	GRANT	Ape	8/22	BEACH	Ape
2/28	HUDDLESTON	Ape	8/29	WINN	Ape
3/7	JAMES	Ape	9/5	WOLFF	Ape
3/14	SULLIVAN *29	Ape	9/12	CLAYTON	Ape
3/21	GOSSETT	Ape	9/19	BATTHYANY	Ape
3/28	FORSTER	Ape	9/26	HUDSON	Ape
4/4	LANSDOWNE	Ape	10/3	CAVE	Ape
4/11	ROEBUCK	Ape	10/10	GORDON	Ape
4/18	WOLSELEY	Ape	10/17	HESSEY	Ape
4/25	HENLEY	Ape	10/24	BRADFORD	Ape
			10/31	ASHBURY	Ape
5/2	FITZGERALD	Ape			
5/9	HARDWICKE	Ape	11/7	LABOUCHERE	Ape
5/16	CROSS	Ape	11/14	SYKES	Ape
5/23	STANHOPE	Ape	11/21	SWINBURNE *30	Ape
5/30	SANDHURST	Ape	11/28	COLENSO *31	Ape
6/6	DEVONSHIRE	Ape	12/5	CHAPLIN	Ape
6/13	BATH	Ape	12/12	HAY	Ape
6/20	ANZEGLIO	Ape	12/19	IRVING *32	Ape
6/27	ADAM	Ape	12/26	WHITE	Ape

*Indicates subject is illustrated in Part I.

Date	Subject	Signed	Date	Subject	Signed
1/2	PUSEY	Ape	7/3	PAGET (A.H.)	Ape
1/9	FRASER	Ape	7/10	STRACEY	Ape
1/16	RUSSELL	Ape	7/17	MILBANK	Ape
1/23	SCHENCK	Ape	7/24	ONSLOW	Ape
1/30	LIDDELL	Ape	7/31	STRADBROKE	Ape
2/6	MÜLLER	Ape	8/7	MUNTZ	Ape
2/13	SCHOUVALOFF	Ape	8/14	WHARNCLIFFE	Ape
2/20	PLAYFAIR	Ape	8/21	BAZLEY	Ape
2/27	REDESDALE	Ape	8/28	BEUST	Ape
3/6	HENDERSON	Ape	9/4	DYKE	Ape
3/13	O'GORMAN	Ape	9/11	BARRINGTON	Ape
3/20	REED	Ape	9/18	PAYNE	Ape
3/27	HENNESSY	Ape	9/25	SALA	Ape
4/3	MOODY *33	Ape	10/2	MATTHEWS	Ape
4/10	SANKEY *34	Ape	10/9	WEBB	Ape
4/17	RAIKES	Ape	10/16	FORESTER	Ape
4/24	JENKINSON	Ape	10/23	HAY	
				(REAR-ADM. JOHN)	Ape
5/1	BURY	Ape	10/30	SAXE-WEIMAR	Ape
5/8	CHEVALIER	Ape			
5/15	LOPES	Ape	11/6	WATKIN	Ape
5/22	SALVINI *35	Ape	11/13	AIRY	Ape
5/29	BUCKINGHAM	Ape	11/20	BROWNING *36	Ape
			11/27	HAYWARD	Ape
6/5	READ	Ape			
6/12	HAY (J.C.D.)	Ape	12/4	LYTTELTON	Ape
6/19	HAMMOND	Ape	12/11	BAGGALLAY	Ape
6/26	ABERGAVENNY	Ape	12/18	GULL	Ape
			12/25	PAGET (C.)	Ape

*Indicates subject is illustrated in Part I.

Date	Subject	Signed	Date	Subject	Signed
1/1	BRETT	Ape	7/1	PORTSMOUTH	Spy
1/8	TWEEDDALE	Ape	7/8	ALINGTON	Spy
1/15	KINNARD	Ape	7/15	CAMERON	Spy
1/22	GOODFORD *37	Spy	7/22	COTTESLOE	Spy
1/29	BRAMWELL	Spy	7/29	TOOLE	Spy
2/5	CLEASBY	Spy	8/5	GULLY	Spy
2/12	PAGET (JAMES)	Spy	8/12	BERESFORD	
2/19	LAWSON	M or JTJ		(CHAS.WM.)	Spy
2/26	JOWETT *38	Spy	8/19	VIVIAN	Spy
			8/26	FARQUHARSON	M or JTJ
3/4	BISCHOFFSHEIM	JTJ			
3/11	TAYLOR	Spy	9/2	LEWIS	Spy
3/18	LYTTON	Spy	9/9	PAGET-SEYMOUR	Spy
3/25	HAINES	M or JTJ	9/16	LIDDON	Spy
			9/23	DUPPLIN	Spy
4/1	MACDONALD	M or JTJ	9/30	BEAUFORT	Spy
4/8	WELLESLEY *39	Spy			
4/15	TORRINGTON	Spy	10/7	COLE	Spy
4/22	KEPPEL	M or JTJ	10/14	JUNG	Spy
4/29	CARLOS VII	Spy	10/21	GEORGE (KING OF	
				GREECE)	Spy
5/6	MIDLETON	Spy	10/28	NEWBRY and MORNE	Spy
5/13	BERESFORD (MARCUS)	Spy			
5/20	RODEN	Spy	11/4	LINDSAY	Spy
5/27	POWIS	Spy	11/11	LONDONDERRY	Spy
			11/18	DE BATHE	Spy
6/3	ROSEBERY	Spy	11/25	STURT	Spy
6/10	ESLINGTON	Spy			
6/17	CONNAUGHT	Spy	12/2	BURNABY	Spy
6/24	HERBERT of		12/9	NORTHBROOK	Spy
	MUCKROSS	Spy	12/16	MACDUFF	Spy
			12/23	MÜNSTER	Spy
			12/30	MELLISH	Spy

*Indicates subject is illustrated in Part I.

Date	Subject	Signed	Date	Subject	Signed
1/6	ANDRASSY	K_?	7/7	MARTIN	Spy
1/13	PRINCEP	Spy	7/14	JOSEPH of FRANCE	Spy
1/20	NEWMAN *40	Spy	7/21	BIGGAR	Spy
1/27	CHAMBERLAIN	Spy	7/28	RUSSELL	Spy
2/3	HORSFORD	Spy	8/4	CLEVELAND	Spy
2/10	TOOTH *41	Spy	8/11	SEYMOUR	Ape
2/17	RICHARDSON—GARDNER	Spy	8/18	LEVESON—GOWER	Spy
2/24	WINCHESTER	Spy	8/25	KNOLLYS	Ape
3/3	CORRY	Spy	9/1	FALMOUTH	Spy
3/10	HAMILTON	Spy	9/8	VILLEBOIS	Ape
3/17	ELLIOT	Spy	9/15	DORÉ	Spy
3/24	DORCHESTER	Spy	9/22	ROTHSCHILD	Ape
3/31	HEADFORT	Spy	9/29	BENSON	Spy
4/7	HERTFORD	Spy	10/6	BRASSEY	Ape
4/14	IGNATIEFF	Spy	10/13	PAGET, G.A.F.	Spy
4/21	LEOPOLD, PRINCE	Spy	10/20	ELLICE	Ape
4/28	BOURKE	Spy	10/27	STEEL	Spy
5/5	BRIGHT	Spy	11/3	MONTAGU	Ape
5/12	DAVENPORT	Spy	11/10	QUEENSBURY	Spy
5/19	WAGNER *42	Spy	11/17	ASTLEY	Spy
5/26	THYNNE	Spy	11/24	DOYLE	Spy
6/2	POTTER	Spy	12/1	SIMMONS	Ape
6/9	GRACE	Spy	12/8	LOWTHER	Spy
6/16	KUO SUNG TAO	Spy	12/15	YOUNG	Ape
6/23	YELVERTON	M or JTJ	12/22	GRIEVE	Spy
6/30	PASHA	Spy	12/29	FRANCIS JOSEPH I	Sue

*Indicates subject is illustrated in Part I.

Date	Subject	Signed	Date	Subject	Signed
1/5	FORBES	Ape	7/2	DISRAELI *45	Ape
1/12	WHISTLER *43	Spy	7/6	ELPHINSTONE	Spy
1/19	WILLIAMS	Ape	7/13	SPOFFORTH	Spy
1/26	PONSONBY-FANE	Spy	7/29	STEELE	Ape
			7/27	HAMILTON	Spy
2/2	RUSSELL	Ape			
2/9	HOLKER	Spy	8/3	HUMBERT of ITALY	T
2/16	FITZMAURICE	Spy	8/10	NORTH	Spy
2/23	LUBBOCK	Spy	8/17	TENTERDEN	Spy
			8/24	PORTARLINGTON	Spy
3/2	DENBIGH	Ape	8/31	JENKINS	Spy
3/9	BAKER PASHA	Ape			
3/16	MARSHALL	Ape	9/7	KENSINGTON	Spy
3/23	DOYLE	Spy	9/14	FITZWILLIAM	Ape
3/30	FEVERSHAM	Ape	9/21	CAMPBELL	Spy
			9/28	WADDINGTON	T
4/6	LYONS	Ape			
4/13	LYSONS	Spy	10/5	GERARD	Spy
4/20	NAPIER of MAGDALA	Spy	10/12	ORMOND	Spy
4/27	COWEN	Spy	10/19	LONDESBOROUGH	Spy
			10/26	TENNIEL	Spy
5/4	DUNRAVEN/MT. EARL	Ape			
5/11	LINDSAY	Spy	11/2	MONTGOMERY	Spy
5/18	POPE LEO XIII	T	11/9	WILSON	Ape
5/25	WELLESLEY	Ape	11/16	YATES	Spy
			11/23	OWEN	Spy
6/1	PASHA (HOBART)	Spy	11/30	MORLEY	Ape
6/8	KEMBALL	Ape			
6/15	GARIBALDI *44	T	12/7	JOHNSTONE	Spy
6/22	GIFFARD	Spy	12/14	DUNMORE	Spy
6/29	LANE-FOX	Spy		PRINCE of WALES	Spy
			12/21	SEELY	Spy
			12/28	MANCHESTER	Spy

*Indicates subject is illustrated in Part I.

Date	Subject	Signed	Date	Subject	Signed
1/4	HARTE	Spy	7/1 {	GLADSTONE	Spy
1/11	BATEMAN			*ROW IN SEASON*	Corbould
1/18	BOWYER	Spy	7/5	BERNHARDT * 46	T?
1/25	RYLANDS	Spy	7/12	GRÉVY	T
			7/19	HUNT	Spy
2/1	GOUNOD	T	7/26	BONAPARTE (JEROME)	T
2/8	OTWAY	Ape			
2/15	VERDI	T	8/2	BROOKS	Spy
2/22	RENAN	T	8/9	WATERFORD	Spy
			8/16	SASSOON	Spy
3/1	JESSEL	Spy	8/23	SYKES	Spy
3/8	EDMONSTONE	Spy	8/30	DELAWARR	Spy
3/15	CREALOCK	Spy			
3/22	TADEMA	Ape	9/6	FRASER	Spy
3/29	HAVELOCK	Spy	9/13	BHASKARAWONGSE	Spy
			9/20	HUGO	T
4/5	HAMILTON	Spy	9/27	BERESFORD (Wm.L.)	Spy
4/12	STANHOPE	Spy			
4/19	HENRY	Spy	10/4	CHENERY	Spy
4/26	SPENCER	CG	10/11	MACMAHON	T
			10/18	BYNG *48	Spy
5/3	SUFFIELD	Ape	10/25	DONOUGHMORE	Spy
5/10	STRAIGHT	Spy			
5/17	MORGAN	Spy	11/1	WILLIAMS	Spy
5/24	STANLEY	Ape	11/8	ATHOLE	Spy
5/31	MILES	Spy	11/15	WOOD	Spy
			11/22	STIRLING—CRAWFURD	Spy
6/7	CASTLEREAGH	Spy	11/29	ELLIOT	Spy
6/14	LONSDALE	Spy			
6/21	LEITH	Spy	12/6	CASSAGNAC	T
6/28	WILLIAMS—WYNN	Spy	12/13	SHELLEY	Ape
			12/16	DISRAELI and CORRY	Spy
			12/20	BLANC	T
			12/27	DUMAS FILS	T

*Indicates subject is illustrated in Part I.

Date	Subject	Signed	Date	Subject	Signed
1/3	SAVILE	Spy	7/3	FOLKESTONE	Ape
1/10	WARD	Spy	7/6	*TREASURY BENCH* *47	T
1/17	GIFFORD	**Spy**	7/10	SPENCER-CHURCHILL	Spy
1/24	ZOLA	T	7/17	SHREWSBURY/TALBOT	Spy
1/31	PALMER	Spy	7/24	PHILLIPS	Ape
			7/31	GORST	Spy
2/7	MACDONALD	Spy			
2/14	KINGSCOTE	Spy	8/7	GUEST	Spy
2/21	WHITLEY	Spy	8/14	FORBES	Ape
2/28	RAMSAY	Spy	8/21	LOWELL	T
			8/28	O'DONNELL	T
3/6	FRASER	Spy			
3/13	CLARKE	Spy	9/4	RICHARD	Spy
3/20	SPOFFORTH	Ape	9/11	PARNELL	T
3/27	INVERURIE	Spy	9/18	ANGLESEY	Ape
			9/25	COURTNEY	T
4/3	HEADLEY	Ape			
4/10	ROBERTS	WGR?	10/2	WINCHILSEA	Spy
4/17	GREGORY	Spy	10/9	AILESBURY	T
4/24	STRACEY	Ape	10/16	SINCLAIR	Ape
			10/23	O'DONAGHUE	Spy
5/1	MEISSONIER	T	10/30	WYNDHAM	Spy
5/8	ARDILAUN	Spy			
5/15	CALCRAFT	Spy	11/6	BESSEMER	Spy
5/22	DE WORMS	Ape	11/13	LYMINGTON	Spy
5/29	PLUNKETT	Ape	11/20	ABOUT	T
			11/27	BASTARD	Spy
6/5	GORDON-CUMMING	Ape			
6/12	BRADLAUGH	Spy	12/1	*THE FOURTH PARTY*	Spy
6/19	GREENWOOD	Ape	12/4	SAY	Ape
6/26	PAGET, A.B.	T	12/11	CARDEN	Spy
			12/18	WILSON	Spy
			12/25	SARDOU	T

*Indicates subject is illustrated in Part I.

Date	Subject	Signed	Date	Subject	Signed
1/1	CONYNGHAM	Spy	7/2	COX	Spy
1/8	BURAND	Spy	7/5	HER MAJESTY'S	
1/15	TEMPLE	Spy		OPPOSITION *50	T
1/22	BOEHM	Spy	7/9	EWART	T
1/29	BOYCOTT	Spy	7/16	HARRIS	Spy
			7/23	RIDLEY	Ape
2/5	CUNARD	Spy	7/30	AVELAND	Spy
2/12	HOWARD	Spy			
2/19	GORDON	Ape	8/6	CLONMELL	Ape
2/26	KENMARE	Spy	8/13	COVENTRY	Ape
			8/20	YORKE	Spy
3/5	HAMILTON	Spy	8/27	PERCY	T
3/12	BARTLETT	Spy			
3/19	HERSCHELL	Spy	9/3	CHELMSFORD	Spy
3/26	RYLE (BIS.		9/10	WALTER	Spy
	LIVERPOOL)	Ape	9/17	FORTESCUE	T
			9/24	MONTAGU-DOUGLAS-	
4/2	WAVENEY	Spy		SCOTT	T
4/9	EXETER	Ape			
4/16	NELSON	Spy	10/1	NORFOLK	Spy
4/23	LUCAN	Spy	10/8	M'ARTHUR	Spy
4/30	TOLLEMACHE	Spy	10/15	RENDLESHAM	T
			10/22	MACCLESFIELD	Spy
5/7	ISMAIL PACHA	T	10/29	LOWTHER	Spy
5/14	ROSE	Spy			
5/21	GILBERT	Spy	11/5	KNIGHTLY	Spy
5/28	ARCHER	Spy	11/12	ROSSLYN	T
			11/19	BLACKBURN	Spy
6/4	CADOGAN	Spy	11/26	HAWARDEN	T
6/11	RIBBLESDALE	Spy			
6/18	BLANFORD	T	12/3	BISSET	Spy
6/25	FOWLER	T		GLADSTONE (Memorial)	
			12/7	FORCE NO REMEDY	
				*49	Furniss
			12/10	SPENCER	Spy
			12/17	LEVEN and	
				MELVILLE	Spy
			12/24	COMMERELL	T
			12/31	FULKE-GREVILLE	Spy

*Indicates subject is illustrated in Part I.

Date	Subject	Signed	Date	Subject	Signed
1/7	CREWE	Spy	7/1	HENNIKER	T
1/14	SMILES	Spy	7/5	*PURSE, PUSSY, PIETY*	T
1/21	COOPER	Spy	7/8	LAWES	T
1/28	BATESON	Spy	7/15	VERNEY	Spy
			7/22	ILCHESTER	Spy
2/4	ROBARTES	Spy	7/29	MILNE	T
2/11	GLADSTONE, W.E.	Spy			
2/18	HOLMS	Spy	8/5	BARNE	Spy
2/25	MUNSTER		8/12	FITZPATRICK	Spy
			8/19	FLOWER	T
3/4	HALDON	Spy	8/26	CETEWAYO	Spy
3/11	LLOYD	Spy			
3/18	MONTROSE	Spy	9/2	FORDHAM	Spy
3/25	PENRHYN	Spy	9/9	WALSINGHAM	T
			9/16	BRUDENELL-BRUCE	Spy
4/1	ERRINGTON	T	9/23	WIMBORNE	T
4/8	MOBBRAY	Spy	9/30	LIDDELL, A.F.O.	Spy
4/15	TOTTENHAM	Spy			
4/22	MANDEVILLE	Spy	10/7	MACDONNELL	Spy
4/29	BRUCE	Spy	10/14	PULESTON	Spy
			10/21	ASHMEAD-BARTLETT	Spy
5/6	GLADSTONE, H.J.	Spy	10/28	ARMISTEAD	Spy
5/13	DILLWYN	Spy			
5/20	SELKIRK	Spy	11/4	ELLIS	Spy
5/27	LECKY	Spy	11/11	EDWARDS	Spy
			11/18	SINGH	Spy
6/3	PORTLAND	Spy	11/25	BOOTH *51	Spy
6/10	SCOTT	Spy			
6/17	ANSTRUTHER-THOMSON	Spy	12/2	FOLEY	Spy
6/24	GOOCH, A.	Ape	12/5	ALEXANDRA (WALES)	Chartran
			12/9	GOOCH, D.	Spy
			12/16	BOUCICAULT	Spy
			12/23	LINDSAY	Spy
			12/30	MALLOCK	Spy

*Indicates subject is illustrated in Part I.

Date	Subject	Signed	Date	Subject	Signed
1/6	ARABI-AHMED	FV	7/7	KINCAID-LENNOX	Spy
1/13	BENNETT	Spy	7/14	ALBEMARLE	T
1/20	TEWFIK-PASHA	FV	7/21	GARDNER	Spy
1/27	VIS. BARING	Spy	7/28	PALMER	Spy
2/3	LINDSAY		8/4	LEICESTER	Spy
2/10	HOZIER		8/11	ROCKSAVAGE	Spy
2/17	CLEVELAND	Chartran	8/18	ONSLOW	Spy
2/24	HOARE	Spy	8/25	FOLEY	Spy
3/3	PROCTOR	Spy	9/1	WATERFORD	Chartran
3/10	BURNABY	T	9/8	MOUNTCASHELL	Spy
3/17	PONSONBY	T	9/15	DIGBY	Spy
3/24	MARRIOTT	T	9/22	STAIR	Spy
3/31	FREAK	T	9/29	SEAFIELD	Spy
4/7	PAUNCEFOTE	T	10/6	LONSDALE, COUNTESS	T
4/14	LT.GEN.CHAS.BARING	T	10/13	COTES	Spy
4/21	VIVIAN	T	10/20	CORBET	Zpy (Spy)
4/28	HILEY-HOSKINS	Spy	10/27	DOWNE	Spy
5/5	RUSSELL	(Verheyden)	11/3	BURDETT-COUTTS	T
5/12	LAWES		11/10	WESTMORELAND	Spy
5/19	FITZGERALD		11/17	ASHLEY	Spy
5/26	WEBSTER		11/24	MILLTOWN	Spy
			11/27	*THE CABINET*	
6/2	THORNHILL			*COUNCIL*	T
6/9	TENNANT	(Ward)			
6/16	DUFF		12/1	DALHOUSIE, COUNTESS	T
6/23	LECHMERE	T	12/8	TORRENS	Spy
6/30	MIDDLETON	T	12/15	QUAIN	Zpy (Spy)
			12/22	VINCENT	Spy
			12/29	FORESTER	Spy

*Indicates subject is illustrated in Part I.
NOTE: Unsigned cartoons this year are by either Verheyden or Jopling.

Date	Subject	Signed	Date	Subject	Signed
1/5	LADY DIXIE	T	7/5	GLEICHEN	Go
1/12	MALET	Spy	7/12	COUPLAND	Ape
1/19	PORTMAN	Spy	7/19	CARTWRIGHT	Spy
1/26	HERKOMER	FG	7/26	STIRLING	Spy
2/2	LADY HOLLAND	T	8/2	SLAGG	Ape
2/9	WYKE	Ape	8/9	BROADHURST	Spy
2/16	SEYMOUR	Spy	8/16	DENNING *53	Ape
2/23	COVENTRY	Spy	8/23	MOLTKE *54	Go
			8/30	BRODRICK	Spy
3/1	TWEEDDALE	T			
3/8	CARDROSS	Spy	9/6	WILLOUGHBY	Spy
3/15	BRAND	Spy	9/13	BONNER	Ape
3/22	HALDON	Spy	9/20	LYTTELTON	Ape
3/29	ROGERS	Spy	9/27	D'AUMALE	Nemo
4/5	ELIZABETH of		10/4	HUBBARD	Spy
	AUSTRIA	C.DeGrimm	10/11	ALEXANDER III,	
4/12	HIGGINSON	Spy		RUSSIA	Nemo
4/19	PARKER	Ape	10/18	PALMER	Ape
4/26	HAAG	Go	10/25	GEORGE	Ape
5/3	WELDON	Spy	11/1	FIRR	Spy
5/10	WARTON	Ape	11/8	KNIGHT	Spy
5/17	HANBURY-TRACY	Spy	11/15	BENNETT	Nemo
5/24	WILDE *52	Ape	11/22	CHAMBERS	Spy
5/31	ROTHSCHILD, A.	Spy	11/29	HANSARD	Ape
6/7	LOUISA, PRINCESS	Nemo	12/6	SMITH, A.	Ape
6/14	NORTHUMBERLAND	Spy	12/13	ROTHSCHILD, L.	Spy
6/21	CURRIE	Ape	12/20	LICHFIELD	
6/28	RAMSDEN	Spy		(BICKERSTETH)	Spy
			12/27	GIERS	Nemo

*Indicates subject is illustrated in Part I.

Date	Subject	Signed	Date	Subject	Signed
1/3	WELLINGTON	Ape	7/4	GIBSON	Spy
1/10	THOROLD (BISH.		7/11	LIMERICK	Ape
	ROCHESTER)	Spy	7/18	ELLICOTT	Spy
1/17	MAHON	Spy	7/25	CALTHORPE	Spy
1/24	WILSON, S.	Spy			
1/31	BLUNT	Ape	8/1	ALLSOPP	Spy
			8/8	LUMSDEN	Spy
2/7	CHETWYND	Spy	8/15	BIRBECK	Ape
2/14	ROSE	Spy	8/22	GRAIN	Spy
2/21	WILSON, C.H.	Ape	8/29	OPFER of BLOWITZ	Ape
2/28	COLEBROOKE	Spy			
			9/5	COTTON	Spy
3/7	STEPHEN	Spy	9/12	CANNON	Spy
3/14	DELACOUR	Spy	9/19	LESSAR	Ape
3/21	ARDITI	Ape	9/26	AKERS—DOUGLAS	Ape
3/28	CHITTY	Spy			
			10/3	HOULDSWORTH	Ape
4/4	ROBERTS	Spy	10/10	PRICE	Spy
4/11	EDIS	Ape	10/17	EDWARDS	Ape
4/18	BRYDGES-WILLIAMS	Spy	10/24	BURTON	Ape
4/25	BAXTER	Spy	10/31	RITCHIE	Ape
5/2	ESCOTT	Ape	11/7	BATESON—HARVEY	Spy
5/9	EARDLY-WILMOT	Spy	11/14	TOSTI	Ape
5/16	PASHA, H.F.	Spy	11/21	NICKALLS	Pat
5/23	McCARTHY	Spy	11/28	HARROWBY	Ape
5/30	JOCELYN	Ape			
			12/5	M. DE STAAL	Ape
6/6	HARRISON	Spy	12/12	POPE, S.	Spy
6/13	SULLIVAN	Ape	12/19	ARTHUR	Spy
6/20	WARRE	Spy	12/26	WILKINSON	Spy
6/27	MILNER	Ape		*NEWMARKET, 1885*	LIB

*Indicates subject is illustrated in Part I.

Date	Subject	Signed	Date	Subject	Signed
1/2	DUCKWORTH	Ape	7/3	CRAVEN	Lib
1/9	KING-HARMAN	Spy	7/10	LONSDALE (H.CECIL)	Spy
1/16	CAIRNS	Spy	7/17	WALROND	Lib
1/23	HARRISON	Ape	7/24	HASTINGS	Lib
1/30	CHURCH	Lib	7/31	ZETLAND	Spy
2/6	WARREN	Ape	8/7	GRAFTON	Spy
2/13	TYRWHITT-WILSON	Spy	8/14	LEVESON-GOWER	Spy
2/20	INGHAM	Spy	8/21	HILL	Spy
2/27	KERR	Spy	8/28	FOUNTAGNE-WILSON-	
				MONTAGU	Spy
3/6	NIGRA	Ape			
3/13	POLAND	Spy	9/4	PECK	Lib
3/20	INNES-KERR	Spy	9/11	STUART-WORTLEY,	
3/27	THORNTON	Ape		C.B.	Spy
			9/18	ELLENBOROUGH	Spy
4/3	HEALY	Spy	9/25	SIMON	Spy
4/10	KENNAWAY	Spy			
4/17	GARDNER	Spy	10/2	CAVENDISH, E.	Spy
4/24	COHEN	Lib	10/9	ROLLIT	Spy
			10/16	LONG	Spy
5/1	BALFOUR	Spy	10/23	BARTTELOT	Spy
5/8	TATTERSALL	Lib	10/30	PERKINS	Hay
5/15	LISZT	Spy			
5/22	WOOD	Lib	11/6	MONTAGU, S.	Lib
5/29	BRABAZON	Ape	11/13	HANSON	Ape
			11/20	STURGE	Spy
6/5	VIVIAN	Spy	11/27	EGERTON of TATTON	Ape
6/12	SELBY	\Spy			
6/19	HOLMES *55	Spy	12/4	DAWSON	Lib
6/26	ARCH	Spy	12/11	HERBERT	Ape
			12/18	HUGHES-HALLETT	Ape
			12/25	POWER	Spy
			Winter No.: *LOBBY, HOUSE*		
			OF COMMONS *57		Lib

*Indicates subject is illustrated in Part I.

Date	Subject	Signed	Date	Subject	Signed
1/1	TRURO (WILDE)	Ape	7/2	PEEL	Spy
1/8	PASTEUR *56	T	7/9	BARKLEY	Spy
1/15	STEWART	Ape	7/16	JOYNES *58	Spy
1/22	ELLESMERE	Ape	7/23	BENZON	Spy
1/29	HOLLAND	Ape	7/30	BENSON, E.W.	Spy
2/5	BROWNE	Ape	8/6	ELTON	Spy
2/12	BUTT	Ape	8/13	MANNERS	Ape
2/19	EBRINGTON	Ape	8/20	LOCKWOOD	Spy
2/26	SAUNDERSON	Ape	8/27	SING, PERTAB	Spy
3/5	COLERIDGE	Ape	9/3	BARRETT	Lib
3/12	BOULANGER	T	9/10	MATTHEWS	Spy
3/19	DUNCAN	Ape	9/17	HEATON	Spy
3/26	COLOMB	Ape	9/24	BALFOUR, A.J.	Spy
4/2	HAMLEY	Ape	10/1	PEASE	Spy
4/9	LYNE (IGNATIUS)	Ape	10/8	GROVE	Spy
4/16	BURGHLEY	Ape	10/15	MACKENZIE	Ape
4/23	GOLDSMID	Ape	10/22	SUTHERLAND	Ape
4/30	FIELD	Spy	10/29	NORTH	Spy
5/7	DILLON	Ape	11/5	GLADSTONE *59	Spy
5/14	CORRY	Ape	11/12	SMITH, W.H.	Spy
5/21	HAGGARD	Spy	11/19	SOMERSET	Spy
5/28	PITT-LEWIS	Spy	11/26	KEYSER	Spy
6/4	MEYSEY-THOMPSON	Ape	12/3	MACHELL	Spy
6/11	HARGREAVES	Spy	12/6	*TATTERSALL'S*	Lib
6/18	STEPHENSON	Spy	12/10	OSBORNE	Lib
6/25	WATTS	Lib	12/17	HENEAGE	Spy
			12/24	DURHAM	Spy
			12/31	SUFFOLK and BERKSHIRE	Lib

*Indicates subject is illustrated in Part I.

Date	Subject	Signed	Date	Subject	Signed
1/7	KAY	Spy	7/7	PHILIPS	Ape
1/14	PAGET, A.V.	Spy	7/14	PENBROKE and	
1/21	GROSSMITH	Spy		MONTGOMERY	Ape
1/28	SMITH, E.J.H.	Hay	7/21	HARTINGTON	Spy
			7/28	READ, W.W.	Lib
2/4	CHARLES, A.	Spy			
2/11	GENNADIUS	Spy	8/4	TANNER	Spy
2/18	HALL	Spy	8/11	LARKING	Ape
2/25	O'CONNOR	Spy	8/18	TEMPLETOWN	Ape
			8/25	BONTINE-C-C-G	Spy
3/3	CHANDOS-POLE	Spy			
3/10	GODFREY	Spy	9/1	BROMLEY-DAVENPORT	Spy
3/17	GOODWIN	Spy	9/8	PAYN	Ape
3/24	RUSSELL, T.W.	Spy	9/15	REVELSTOKE	Lib
3/31	PICKERSGILL	Spy	9/22	HAWEIS	Ape
			9/29	BRADLEY	Spy
4/7	AILESBURY	Lib			
4/14	CATHCART	Spy	10/6	BAIRD	Lib
4/21	HANNEN	Spy	10/13	PRINCE ALBERT	Hay
4/28	READ, J.F.H.	Lib	10/20	BESSBOROUGH	Spy
			10/27	DAY	Spy
5/5	COMBERMERE	Spy			
5/12	BATES	Spy	11/3	SMITH, A.L.	Spy
5/19	COTTON	Spy	11/10	RODNEY	Lib
5/26	BRAND	Lib	11/17	CROSSLEY	Spy
			11/24	BROWNING	Hay
6/2	BLACKBURNE	Ape			
6/9	ROTHSCHILD, N.	Lib	12/1	COLLINGS	Spy
6/16	FLOQUET	Ape	12/8	THE WINNING POST	Lib
6/23	MACDONALD	Spy	12/15	FINLAY	Ape
6/30	GILBEY	Spy	12/22	DALBY	Ape
			12/29	KENYON	Spy

Date	Subject	Signed	Date	Subject	Signed
1/5	CHURCHILL, R.H.S.	Lib	7/6	SOLTYKOFF	Spy
1/12	DANGAN	Spy	7/13	BOWLES *61	Spy
1/19	MORGAN, E.H.	Hay	7/20	NICKALLS	Spy
1/26	MORGAN, H.A.	Hay	7/27	FIFE	Spy
2/2	GRIMTHROPE	Spy	8/3	COMMERELL	Spy
2/9	QUILTER	Lib	8/10	WEBB	Lib
2/16	ROBERTSON	Spy	8/17	HOTHFIELD	Spy
2/23	CARMARTHEN	Hay	8/24	EGERTON	Lib
			8/31	COATES	Spy
3/2	RUSSELL	Spy			
3/9	PIGOTT	Spy	9/7	SEARLE	Spy
3/16	WHITEHEAD	Hay	9/14	CORLETT	Spy
3/23	MACKENZIE of		9/21	CARNOT	Pal
	KINTAIL	Lib	9/28	HARRIS	Spy
3/30	DROGHEDA	Hay			
			10/5	McCALMONT	Spy
4/6	BRIGHT	Ape	10/12	PORTER	Lib
4/13	GOURAUD	Ape	10/19	GRENFELL	Spy
4/20	ALLSOPP	Lib	10/26	DEPEW	Spy
4/27	PELLEGRINI *61	A.J.Marks			
			11/2	NORTH	Spy
5/4	MURPHY	Spy	11/9	ISAACS	Spy
5/11	EIFFEL	Guth	11/16	BARNUM *62	Spy
5/18	BUTLER	Hay	11/23	WARD *63	Pal
5/25	SARASATE	Ape	11/30	MANISTY	Quiz
6/1	BARRETT	Lib	12/7	BLOWITZ	Guth
6/8	MARKS	AJM	12/14	BROADLEY	Spy
6/15	ROTHSCHILD, F.	Hay	12/21	BARRY	Lib
6/22	SANDHURST	Spy	12/28	CECIL, A.	Spy
6/29	PHILIPSON	Spy			

*Indicates subject is illustrated in Part I.

Date	Subject	Signed	Date	Subject	Signed
1/4	FENTON	Spy	7/5	MITCHELL	Spy
1/11	PIGOTT	Pal	7/12	TREE	Spy
1/18	STUART-WORTLEY	Spy	7/19	HUTCHINSON	Spy
1/25	PIXLEY	Spy	7/26	HIRSCH	Lib
2/1	HILL	Spy	8/2	CONNAUGHT and	
2/8	LINDLEY	Spy		STRATHEARN	Spy
2/15	GREY	Spy	8/9	POLLOCK	Quiz
2/22	GOULD	Lib	8/16	FORWOOD	Lib
			8/23	JARDINE	Spy
3/1	HARE	Spy	8/30	BOURKE	FCG
3/8	LENG	Spy			
3/15	GRANTHAM	Spy	9/6	MILLER	Lib
3/22	MUTTLEBURY	Spy	9/13	LINCOLN (KING)	Spy
3/29	RUSSELL	Quiz	9/20	SASSOON	Spy
			9/27	HUTCHINSON	Spy
4/5	ANGLE	F.C.G.			
4/12	ORLEANS	Guth	10/4	LOATES	Spy
4/19	JAFFRAY	Spy	10/11	JERSEY	Spy
4/26	BERESFORD, M.	Lib	10/18	MILNER, M.H.	Lib
			10/25	VAUGHAN	Spy
5/3	BROOKE	Spy			
5/10	REEVES	Spy	11/1	SAVORY *64	Spy
5/17	WEATHERBY	Lib	11/8	HALSBURY	Spy
5/24	WALES, PRINCE		11/15	BRADFORD	Spy
	GEO. of	Spy	11/22	GREEN	Spy
5/31	CRISP	Spy	11/29	IN VANITY	(by Spy
				FAIR *66	& Others)
6/7	WALKER, A.B.	Lib			
6/14	MONRO	Spy	12/6	KENNARD	Lib
6/21	WOODBURN	Spy	12/13	WILLIAMS	Quiz
6/28	DEACON	Spy	12/20	GRENFELL	Spy
			12/27	HOULDSWORTH	Spy

*Indicates subject is illustrated in Part I.

Date	Subject	Signed	Date	Subject	Signed
1/3	MAGNUS	S.TEL	7/4	MOROCCO	Spy
1/10	WILSON	Spy	7/11	IVEAGH	Spy
1/17	COCK	Stuff	7/18	FIELD	Spy
1/24	DORMER	Bint	7/25	BIDDULPH	Spy
1/31	GROVE	Spy			
			8/1	ASQUITH *65	Spy
2/7	WARMINGTON	Stuff	8/8	RESZKE	Spy
2/14	CARTE	Spy	8/15	HORNBY	Stuff
2/21	BLACK	Spy	8/22	PLAT	Spy
2/28	D'AUMALE	Guth	8/28	STAINER	Spy
3/7	PINERO	Spy	9/5	YORK (ARCHBSHP.	
3/14	KNOLLYS	Spy		MALLAGAN)	Spy
3/21	AMPTHILL	Spy	9/12	BEERS	Spy
3/28	RHODES, C.	Spy	9/19	HARRINGTON	Lib
			9/26	FOSTER	Spy
4/4	SCOTTER	Spy			
4/11	JEUNE	Stuff	10/3	EATON	Spy
4/18	FREYCINET	Guth	10/10	FARRAR	Spy
4/25	BRIDGE	Spy	10/17	JOHORE SULTAN	Kyo
			10/24	CANNON	Spy
5/2	SARDOU	Guth	10/31	EDLIN	Spy
5/9	GILL	Spy			
5/16	PAVY	Spy	11/7	WILLIAMS	Spy
5/23	BEARD	Spy	11/14	GLADSTONE, J.H.	Spy
5/30	FRY	Spy	11/21	BIDDULPH, M.A.S.	Spy
			11/28	OWEN	Spy
6/6	MAPLE	Spy			
6/13	BANCROFT	Spy	12/5	*BENCH AND BAR*	Stuff
6/20	AIRD	Spy	12/12	ROMER	Stuff
6/27	WRIGHT	Stuff	12/19	LOWTHER	Spy
			12/26	WATTS	Spy

*Indicates subject is illustrated in Part I.

Date	Subject	Signed	Date	Subject	Signed
1/2	GURDON	Stuff	7/2	SCHNADHORST	Stuff
1/9	LURGAN	Spy	7/9	STODDART	Stuff
1/16	SAMBOURNE	Spy	7/16	WEST	Spy
1/23	SMITH, C.C.	Kyo	7/23	MUNTZ	Spy
1/30	HALE	Spy	7/30	COOKE	Spy
2/6	MATHEWS	Spy	8/6	WOODS	Stuff
2/13	AINGER	Spy	8/13	WEST	Spy
2/20	THORNYCROFT	Spy	8/20	LAMINGTON	Spy
2/27	GORDON-LENNOX	Spy	8/27	BRAMWELL	Spy
3/5	BALL	Lib	9/3	JACKSON	Spy
3/12	BOWEN	Spy	9/10	DALRYMPLE	Spy
3/19	BALFOUR, J.S.	Spy	9/17	NORTON	Spy
3/26	ELCHO	Spy	9/24	HAWKE	Spy
4/2	JONES, H.A.	Spy	10/1	WILKS	Spy
4/9	CARTER	Stuff	10/8	KEAY	Spy
4/16	WIGGIN	Stuff	10/15	BURNS	Spy
4/23	MAJENDIE	Spy	10/22	MACLURE	Spy
4/30	FERGUSSON	Spy	10/29	FINDLAY	Spy
5/7	STURT	Spy	11/5	HOWARD	Spy
5/14	BYNG	Stuff	11/12	REDMOND	Spy
5/21	HAWTREY	Spy	11/19	DENMAN	Stuff
5/28	BRUCE	Spy	11/26	HENLEY	Spy
6/4	HARDY *65	Spy	12/3	MIXED POLITICAL WARES *69	
6/11	HERMAN-HODGE	Spy			Spy
6/18	CURZON	Spy	12/10	HOUGHTON	Spy
6/25	LLOYD	Lib	12/17	METHUEN	Spy
			12/24	FILDES	Spy
			12/31	POLLOCK	Spy

*Indicates subject is illustrated in Part I.

Date	Subject	Signed	Date	Subject	Signed
1/7	WESTMINSTER (NAUGHAN)	Spy	7/6	VICTORIA MARY	Leslie Ward
1/14	COLLINS	Quiz	7/13	HAMOND	Spy
1/21	ALPHONSO VIII		7/20	HASTIE	Spy
1/28	WENLOCK	Bint	7/27	VINE	Spy
			8/3	COQUELIN	Guth
2/4	BEAUREPAIRE	Guth	8/10	PAYNE—GALLWEY	Spy
2/11	CARR	Spy	8/17	WINANS	VA
2/18	BARNES	Spy	8/24	MASCAGNI *70	Lib
2/25	BRYLE	Stuff	8/31	RIGBY	Stuff
3/4	CARINGTON	Spy	9/7	BEAUFORT	Spy
3/11	DAUDET	Guth	9/14	MORRIS	Spy
3/18	FLETCHER	Spy	9/21	NEWTON	Spy
3/25	LOPES	Quiz	9/28	MAXWELL	Spy
4/1	BELLAMY	Spy	10/5	ELLISON—MACARTNEY	Spy
4/8	WARREN	Spy	10/12	BOLTON	Spy
4/13	COZENS—HARDY *68	Spy	10/19	YERBURGH	Spy
4/20	KENDAL	Spy	10/26	ALLAN	Spy
4/27	SOMERSET	Spy			
			11/2	MORGAN	Spy
5/4	CATENA	Hay	11/9	CARSON	Lib
5/11	GRAHAM	Spy	11/16	LAWSON	Spy
5/18	HUNT	Spy	11/23	WILLS	Spy
5/25	VIRCHOW	Spy	11/30	ON THE TERRACE *72	Spy
6/1	SIVEWRIGHT	Spy			
6/8	CRISP	Spy	12/7	CAVE	Spy
6/15	MORTON	Spy	12/14	KENNEDY	Spy
6/22	PENLEY	Spy	12/21	DARNLEY	Spy
6/29	THRING	Spy	12/28	DECRAIS	Guth

*Indicates subject is illustrated in Part I.

Date	Subject	Signed	Date	Subject	Signed
1/4	MICHAILOVITCH	Wag	7/5	LOCH	Spy
1/11	BLAKE	Spy	7/12	TWEEDMOUTH	Spy
1/8	HARRISON	Spy	7/19	BRAND	Spy
1/25	BRETTON	Spy	7/26	ASTLEY	Spy
2/1	CONGLETON	Spy	8/2	DE LaRUE	Spy
2/8	MACDONA	Spy	8/9	LEYLAND	Spy
2/15	CUST	Spy	8/16	PORTARLINGTON	Spy
2/22	ALEXANDER	Spy	8/23	DENBIGH	Spy
			8/30	CASIMIR-PERIER	Guth
3/1	MAGUIRE	Spy			
3/8	TRELOAR	Spy	9/6	LOCKWOOD	Spy
3/15	COTTON	Spy	9/13	BREADALBANE	Spy
3/22	FOGG-ELLIOTT	Spy	9/20	ROTHSCHILD, A.	Guth
3/29	STANLEY	Spy	9/27	GOULD	Spy
4/5	SEWELL	Spy	10/4	ALBERMARLE	Spy
4/12	ERSKINE	Spy	10/11	FOSTER	Spy
4/19	FRY	Spy	10/18	McDONNELL	Spy
4/26	SELOUS	VA	10/25	MILLAR	Spy
5/3	SEFTON	Lib	11/1	BARNBY	Spy
5/10	CLARK	Spy	11/8	ARMSTRONG	Spy
5/17	SANDERSON	Spy	11/15	ISMAY	Lib
5/24	ELLIS	Spy	11/22	PAGET, F.	Spy
5/31	NEWNES	Spy	11/29	FREMANTLE	Pat
6/7	KIPLING	Spy	12/6	*AT COWES* *73	Spy
6/14	MOTT	Spy	12/13	THOMAS	Spy
6/21	THARP	Spy	12/20	SHORTER	Spy
6/28	BAYARD	Spy	12/27	HART	Spy

*Indicates subject is illustrated in Part I.

Date	Subject	Signed	Date	Subject	Signed
1/3	BERESFORD	Spy	7/4	SHEARMAN	Wag
1/10	REID	Spy	7/11	HOWORTH	Spy
1/17	LEHMANN	Spy	7/18	HOLE	F.T.D.
1/24	KEKEWICH	Spy	7/25	BETHELL	Spy
1/31	COURCEL	Guth			
			8/1	BOSON	Guth
2/7	HAMILTON	Spy	8/8	WHITBREAD	Spy
2/14	BARNATO	Spy	8/15	THOMPSON	Spy
2/21	MAY	Spy	8/22	JAY	Spy
2/28	PENROSE-FITZGERALD	Spy	8/29	STRAUSS *71	EBN
			9/5	BALDWIN	Spy
3/7	METTERNICH	Spy	9/12	SANDEMAN	Spy
3/14	CAMPERDOWN	Spy	9/19	FORTESQUE	Spy
3/21	POWELL	Spy	9/26	HARCOURT	Spy
3/28	PITMAN	Spy			
			10/3	COLVILE	Spy
4/4	CAIRD *74	Spy	10/10	DARTMOUTH	Stuff
4/11	GARNETT	Spy	10/17	KEPPEL	Spy
4/18	FAURE	Guth	10/24	PAULTON	Spy
4/25	MAHAVAJIRAVUDH	Spy	10/31	MACNAGHTEN	Spy
5/2	FORBES-ROBERTSON	Spy	11/7	CALVERT	Spy
5/9	CAVENDISH	Spy	11/14	DUCHESNE	Guth
5/16	HARMSWORTH	Spy	11/21	DERRY	Spy
5/23	HATHERTON	Spy	11/28	MASTERS' MEET	Spy
5/30	FARQUHARSON	Spy			
			12/5	PAXTON	Spy
6/6	LOTI	Guth	12/12	CHRISTIAN of DENMARK	Spy
6/13	MANNS	Spy			
6/20	WROTTESLEY	Stuff	12/19	LUGARD	Spy
6/27	BEACH	Spy	12/26	HAWINS	Spy

*Indicates subject is illustrated in Part I.

Date	Subject	Signed	Date	Subject	Signed
1/2	YARBOROUGH	Spy	7/2	CAINE	JBP
1/9	McCALMONT	Spy	7/9	JOHNSTONE	Spy
1/16	EGLINGTON and		7/16	MITCHELL	Spy
	WILTON	Spy	7/23	McIVER	Spy
1/23	DU MAURIER	Spy	7/30	INDERWICK	Spy
1/30	BYRNE	Spy			
			8/6	FELLOWES	Spy
2/6	LONDONDERRY		8/13	LI HUNG CHANG	Guth
	(STEWART)	FTD	8/20	MARCH	Spy
2/13	HALDANE	Spy	8/27	GUEST	Spy
2/20	AUSTIN *75	Spy			
2/27	AMES	Spy	9/3	FOX	Spy
			9/10	BEDFORD	Spy
3/5	BOURCHIER	Spy	9/17	GULLY	Spy
3/12	MATHEW	Spy	9/24	MEREDITH *76	Max
3/19	CRUM	Spy			
3/26	FITZHERBERT	Spy	10/1	Mac CORMAC	Spy
			10/8	DOUGLASS-SCOTT-	
4/2	RASCH	Spy		MONTAGU	Spy
4/9	JAMESON	Spy	10/15	WOODALL	Spy
4/16	OLIPHANT	Spy	10/22	MURRAY	Spy
4/23	BATH	Spy	10/29	GARTH *78	Spy
4/30	HELDER	Spy			
			11/5	LOATES	Spy
5/7	EVANS	Spy	11/12	HANOTAUX	Guth
5/14	JELF	Spy	11/19	CLARKE	Spy
5/21	WALKER	"W.G.Miller"	11/26	ON THE	
5/28	HANBURY	Spy		HEATH *77	Spy
6/4	CURZON	Spy	12/3	DE BROKE	Spy
6/11	CYCLING IN		12/10	BALFOUR, G.	Spy
	HYDE PARK	Halhurst	12/17	HOOLEY	Spy
6/18	DE LA WARR	G.G.Sackville	12/24	MARSHALL	Spy
6/25	WILLS	Spy	12/31	LEACH	F.T.D.

*Indicates subject is illustrated in Part I.

Date	Subject	Signed	Date	Subject	Signed
1/7	RODD	Spy	7/1	RIDLEY	Spy
1/14	WATSON	Spy	7/8	TALBOT, J.G.	Spy
1/21	MOORE	Sic	7/15	DARLING	Spy
1/28	STIRLING	Spy	7/22	TALBOT, R.	Spy
			7/29	MENELIK II	Glick
2/4	PEMBERTON	Spy			
2/11	CAILLARD	Spy	8/5	CROCKETT	F.R.
2/18	JOHNSTON	Spy	8/12	NUGENT	Spy
2/25	ZANGWILL	Sic	8/19	LAURIER	Spy
			8/26	RANJITSINHJI	Spy
3/4	POYNTER	Spy			
3/11	MAUDE	Spy	9/2	WARKWORTH	Spy
3/18	LAWRENCE	Spy	9/9	WINGATE	Spy
3/25	JOHNSTONE	Spy	9/16	SPRIGG	Spy
			9/23	LASCELLES	Spy
4/1	JORDAN	Spy	9/30	HENRY of ORLEANS	Guth
4/8	McLEAN	Spy			
4/15	MILNER	Spy	10/7	FORREST	IMP
4/22	BISH.LONDON		10/14	ANSTRUTHER	Spy
	(MANDELL)	F.T.D.	10/21	NICHOLAS II	Guth
4/29	KELVIN	Spy	10/28	DUNGARVAN	Spy
5/6	TRITTON	Spy	11/4	BACON	Spy
5/13	DICKENS	Spy	11/11	GUEST	C.G.
5/20	JEPHSON	Spy	11/18	BHOWNAGGREE	Spy
5/27	LEGGE, BIS.		11/25	*EMPIRE MAKERS AND*	
	LICHFIELD	Stuff		*BREAKERS*	Stuff
6/3	*AU BOIS DE*		12/2	HOLLMAN	C.G.
	BOULOGNE (AUX		12/9	BEERBOHM *79	Sic
	CHALETS DU CYCLE)	Stuff	12/16	JACKSON	Spy
6/13	PHILLIPS	Spy	12/23	ROBINS	Spy
6/17	QUEEN VICTORIA	Guth	12/30	COOPER	Spy
6/24	HAY	Spy			

*Indicates subject is illustrated in Part I.

Date	Subject	Signed	Date	Subject	Signed
1/6	FALMOUTH	Spy	7/7	HELY-HUTCHINSON	Spy
1/13	GLEICHEN *81	Spy	7/14	BURDETT	Quiz
1/20	BOURKE	Spy	7/21	ECKARDSTEIN	Spy
1/27	MÉLINE	Guth	7/28	HAIG	Gaf
2/3	BIGHAM	Spy	8/4	DEANE	Spy
2/10	SOVERAL	Spy	8/11	REVELSTOKE	Spy
2/17	CHANNEL	Spy	8/18	CORREA	Spy
2/24	DEYM	Spy	8/25	WYNYARD	CG
3/3	RUTHERFORD	Spy	9/1	MOSLEY	Spy
3/10	SNEYD	Stuff	9/8	LOCKHART	Spy
3/17	WITT	Spy	9/15	HALL	Spy
3/24	ORCHARDSON	Spy	9/22	MARLBOROUGH	Spy
3/31	BEATTY	Gaf	9/29	BROOKFIELD	Spy
4/7	BARTON	Spy	10/6	BRISSON	Guth
4/14	RHODES, C.	Spy	10/12	RIMINGTON	Gaf
4/21	SPOONER	Spy	10/20	MAUREL	Spy
4/28	GREY	Spy	10/27	FLETCHER	Spy
5/5	COQUELIN	Guth	11/3	PORTMAN *80	Spy
5/12	MALCOLM	Spy	11/10	SANDERSON	Spy
5/19	EYTON	FTD	11/17	WELDON	Spy
5/26 {	ESTERHAZY	Guth	11/24	PHILLIMORE	Spy
	GLADSTONE	Ape			
			12/1	LORD PROTECT US	} Harry Furniss
6/2	FARQUHAR	Spy	12/8	GREENWELL	Spy
6/9	MORAY	Spy	12/15	BARNARD	Gaf
6/16	HIGGINS	Spy	12/22	HANNAY	Spy
6/23	DANCKWERTS	Spy	12/29	ABBEY	Spy
6/30	BONSOR	Spy			

*Indicates subject is illustrated in Part I.

Date	Subject	Signed	Date	Subject	Signed
1/5	GALWAY	Spy	7/6	BERESFORD	Cloister
1/12	BACKHOUSE	Gaf	7/13	WARD	Spy
1/19	BROOKE	Spy	7/20	BEAUCHAMP	Spy
1/26	LAURENCE	Spy	7/27	MUCK *83	Wag
2/2	McKINLEY	Flagg	8/3	CHAMBERLAIN, A.	Spy
2/9	DELCASSE	Guth	8/10	CAMPBELL-	
2/16	HAMILTON(EDWARD)	Hodge		BANNERMAN	Spy
2/23	KITCHNER	Spy	8/17	LUSHINGTON	Spy
			8/24	COOK	Spy
3/2	WILLIAMS, R.L.	CGD	8/31	JACKSON	Spy
3/9	CAMBON	Guth			
3/16	WHITE	Spy	9/7	DREYFUS	Guth
3/23	GOLD	Spy	9/14	VALENTIA	Spy
3/30	HARGREAVES	CG	9/21	WOOD	Gaf
			9/28	CHOATE	Spy
4/6	TAILBY	Gaf			
4/13	BALFOUR, J.B.	Spy	10/5	STUART	Stuff
4/20	VINCENT	Spy	10/12	DION *84	Guth
4/27	HUNTER	Spy	10/19	LI HSI	Pry
			10/26	STUART-WORTLEY	Spy
5/4	GREENALL	CB			
5/11	HARCOURT *82	Cloister	11/2	FOWLER	FTD
5/18	LOUBET	Guth	11/9	CECIL, E.H.	Spy
5/25	SLOAN	GDG	11/16	HOLFORD	Spy
			11/23	AT RENNES *86	Guth
6/1	VICTOR NAPOLEON	Guth	11/30	STEVENSON	Wag
6/8	RHODES, F.W.	Spy			
6/15	SLATIN	Spy	12/7	CASSEL	Spy
6/22	BALCARRES	Spy	12/14	LUCAS	N
6/29	FLEMING	Spy	12/21	RAYLEIGH	FTD
			12/28	PADEREWSKI *85	Spy

*Indicates subject is illustrated in Part I.

Date	Subject	Signed	Date	Subject	Signed
1/4	BAHADUR *87	MR	7/5	BADEN-POWELL	Drawl
1/11	YATES	Cloister	7/12	FRENCH *89	GDG
1/18	BULLER	Spy	7/19	TREVES	Spy
1/25	NEELD	Cloister	7/26	MADDEN	GDG
2/1	SASSOON	Spy	8/2	ROTHSCHILD, A.	Spy
2/8	FABER	Stuff	8/9	STEYN	Wag
2/15	PYNE	Spy	8/16	RUTZEN	Wag
2/22	FORBES	Spy	8/23	REIFF, J.	Spy
			8/30	REIFF, L.	Spy
3/1	LOWTHER	Spy			
3/8	KRUGER	Drawl	9/6	BIGGE	Spy
3/15	CHESHAM	Spy	9/13	ROTHSCHILD, W.L.	Spy
3/22	THORNTON	Spy	9/20	WYNDHAM	Spy
3/29	WARD	Spy	9/27	CHURCHILL, W. *90	Spy
4/5	BUCKLEY	Spy	10/4	MOULTON	Spy
4/12	YORKE-DAVIS	Spy	10/11	DILLWYN-LLEWELYN	Spy
4/19	STRATHCONA and		10/18	CECIL, H.	Spy
	MT. ROYAL	Spy	10/25	BURNS-HARTOPP	CB
4/26	CAVENDISH	Spy			
			11/1	ALVERSTONE	Spy
5/3	FISHER	Spy	11/8	KERR, W.	Spy
5/10	BUCKNILL	Spy	11/15	FARWELL	FTD
5/17	HOPETOUN	Spy	11/22	KERR, R.	Spy
5/24	CLANRICHARDE	Spy	11/29	A GENERAL GROUP	Spy
5/31	GREVILLE	Spy			
			12/6	BRUCE	Spy
6/7	ALBERT H. CHARLES		12/13	DAWSON	Spy
	of MONACO	Spy	12/20	SALISBURY	Spy
6/14	WHITE	Spy	12/27	WELBY	CB
6/21	ROBERTS *88	Spy			
6/28	LAMBTON	Spy			

*Indicates subject is illustrated in Part I.

Date	Subject	Signed	Date	Subject	Signed
1/3	BARODA	MR	7/4	DEHAVILLAND	Spy
1/10	CLARENDON	Spy	7/11	LEGARD	CB
1/17	HENEAGE	Spy	7/18	BRODRICK	Spy
1/24	COZENS-HARDY	Spy	7/25	JESSOP	Spy
1/31	{ HORNBY	Spy			
	QUEEN VICTORIA *91	Guth	8/1	JAMESON	Spy
			8/8	FITZGERALD	Spy
2/7	MACKINNON	Spy	8/15	SOUTHWELL	Spy
2/14	RAGLAN	Spy	8/22	LAGDEN	Spy
2/21	POLE-CAREW	Spy	8/29	KELLY-KENNY	Spy
2/28	AINGER	Spy			
			9/5	LYTTLETON, N.	Spy
3/7	CHAMBERLAIN, J.	Spy	9/12	RICKABY	Spy
3/14	ROSEBERY	Spy	9/19	LIPTON	Spy
3/21	BAKER	Wag	9/26	WARRE-CORNISH	Spy
3/28	RIGBY	Spy			
			10/3	SELBORNE	Spy
4/4	HARDWICKE	Spy	10/10	MacDONALD	Spy
4/11	PLOWDEN	Wag	10/17	WEATHERBY	Spy
4/18	MIDDLETON	Spy	10/24	TOLSTOI *92	Snapp
4/25	RAWSON	Spy	10/31	SEYMOUR	Spy
5/2	HAMILTON	Spy	11/7	BUTCHER	Spy
5/9	LYTTLETON, E.	Spy	11/14	DUMONT *93	Geo.Hum.
5/16	WHITMORE	Spy	11/21	BOSANQUET	Spy
5/23	INGRAM	Spy	11/28	KIRBY GATE *95	CB
5/30	WARD	Spy			
			12/5	SMITH-DORRIEN	Spy
6/6	LEIGH	Spy	12/12	IBSEN *94	Snapp
6/13	ANSON	Spy	12/19	WINCHESTER	Spy
6/20	ROSTAND	Guth	12/26	BAHADUR	
6/27	WALKER	Spy			

*Indicates subject is illustrated in Part I.

Date	Subject	Signed	Date	Subject	Signed
1/2	CROMER	Spy	7/3	DOUGLAS	Spy
1/9	TROTTER	Spy	7/10	BELL	Spy
1/16	DESART	Spy	7/17	FREDERICK of TECK	Spy
1/23	JOYCE	Spy	7/24	WALTON, J.	Spy
1/30	PAGET	CB	7/31	DE WET	EBN
2/6	ABERDEEN	Spy	8/7	GERVAIS	Guth
2/13	EADY	Spy	8/14	BURLEIGH	Spy
2/20	STONE	Spy	8/21	VILLIERS	Spy
2/27	SANTLEY	Spy	8/28	JACKSON *97	Spy
3/6	WALTON	Spy	9/4	ROOSEVELT *98	Flagg
3/13	MacNEILL	Spy	9/11	TEMPLE (CANTERBURY)	Spy
3/20	SPICER	Spy	9/18	MARKHAM	Spy
3/27	LASCELLES	Spy	9/25	REID, W.	Spy
4/3	COMPTON	Spy	10/2	DIOSY	Spy
4/10	CRIPPS	Spy	10/9	POLLOCK	Spy
4/17	SEDDON	?	10/16	BARTON	Spy
4/24	HAYASKI	Spy	10/23	DIMSDALE *99	Spy
			10/30	BROADBENT	Spy
5/1	SEMON	Spy			
5/8	DUNDONALD	Spy	11/6	FISHER	Spy
5/15	DEVONSHIRE	Spy	11/13	PLUMER	Spy
5/22	JEPHSON	Spy	11/20	WILKINSON	Spy
5/29	TECK	Spy	11/27	HEADS OF LAW *100	Spy
6/5	ABEL	Spy	12/4	DURNFORD	Spy
6/12	CHARLES of		12/11	McEWAN	Spy
	DENMARK	Spy	12/18	STEPHEN	Spy
6/19	EDWARD VII *96	Spy	12/25	FORESTIER-WALKER	Spy
6/26	VICTOR EMMANUEL				
	III	Lib			

*Indicates subject is illustrated in Part I.

Date	Subject	Signed	Date	Subject	Signed
1/1	DAWSON	Spy	7/2	BURGE	Spy
1/8	PIRRIE	Spy	7/9	FULTON	Spy
1/15	HERBERT	Spy	7/16	HILTON	Spy
1/22	CLANWILLIAM	Spy	7/23	SHAND	Spy
1/29	MUZAFFER-ED-DIN	Spy	7/30	SHREWSBURY and TALBOT	Spy
2/5	GREY	Spy			
2/12	RAS MAKUNAN	Spy	8/6	PALAIRET	Spy
2/19	LAKING	Spy	8/13	HUTTON	Jest
2/26	KENSINGTON	Spy	8/20	HIRST	Spy
			8/27	BROADWOOD	Spy
3/5	WELLINGTON	Spy			
3/12	CHANG TA-JEN	Spy	9/3	WARNER	Spy
3/19	OWENS	Spy	9/10	MAHER	Ao
3/26	MAY	Spy	9/17	SCOTT	Spy
			9/24	HALL	Spy
4/1	CHAPMAN	Spy			
4/9	HUGGINS	Spy	10/1	WATTS	Ao
4/16	COVENTRY	Cloister	10/8	DE BILLE	Spy
4/23	SATOW	Spy	10/15	KEPPEL	Ao
4/30	PORTMAN-DALTON	Cloister	10/22	LETCHWORTH	Spy
			10/29	CARNEGIE	Spy
5/7	KUBELIK	Spy			
5/14	DEICHMAN *101	Spy	11/5	WILMOT	Ao
5/21	CROOKES	Spy	11/12	AOSTA	Lib
5/28	BUTLER	Spy	11/19	McCALL	Spy
			11/26	HOOD	Spy
6/4	BENSON	Spy			
6/11	CLARKE	Spy	12/3	BEDFORD	Spy
6/18	FERGUSSON	Spy	12/10	PIUS X	Lib
6/25	NORMAN	Spy	12/17	PEEL	Spy
			12/24	DE BENCKENDORFF	Spy
			12/31	BEATTY	GDG

*Indicates subject is illustrated in Part I.

Date	Subject	Signed	Date	Subject	Signed
1/7	BECKETT	Spy	7/7	REDMOND	Spy
1/14	MACKENZIE	Spy	7/14	ASQUITH	Spy
1/21	CHURCHILL	Spy	7/21	LALAING	Spy
1/28	GOLDMANN	Spy	7/28	INVERCLYDE	Spy
2/4	LODGE	Spy	8/4	SMITH, S.	Spy
2/11	NORTHAMPTON	Spy	8/11	HEMPHILL	Spy
2/18	ISAACS	Spy	8/18	SHUTTLEWORTH	Spy
2/25	DE MACLEAN	Spy	8/25	HOLLAND	Spy
3/3	NORTHCOTE	Spy	9/1	DOHERTY	Spy
3/10	AMHERST	Spy	9/8	HUTCHINSON	Spy
3/17	LAMBTON	Spy	9/15	BOSANQUET	Spy
3/24	SHEPPARD	Spy	9/22	DALMENY	Spy
3/31	ADLER	Spy	9/29	JONES *103	Ao
4/7	DARNLEY	Spy	10/6	DUNCANNON	Spy
4/14	BRIDGE	Spy	10/13	WALLER	Imp
4/21	ROCHESTER	Spy	10/20	JEBB	Spy
4/28	POWELL	Spy	10/27	EUSTACE-JAMESON	Spy
5/5	COBHAM	Spy	11/3	WINCHESTER	Spy
5/12	DURAND	Spy	11/10	AGA KHAN	Spy
5/19	JELF	Spy	11/17	PEARSON	Spy
5/26	JAMES	Spy	11/24	CAMPBELL *102	Spy
6/2	AVORY	Spy	12/1	SCOTT-GATTY	Spy
6/9	CAYZER	Spy	12/8	SMITH, W.F.D.	Spy
6/16	REDESDALE	Spy	12/15	MAXIM *104	Spy
6/23	STIRLING-STUART	Spy	12/22	M. and MME. CURIE *105	Imp
6/30	ROSE	Spy	12/29	RODIN *106	Imp

*Indicates subject is illustrated in Part I.

Date	Subject	Signed	Date	Subject	Signed
1/5	JOACHIM	Spy	7/6	RAWLE	Spy
1/12	LANKESTER *107	Spy	7/13	BAGGALLAY	Spy
1/19	THORNYCROFT	Spy	7/20	CAILLARD	Guth
1/26	WOLFE-BARR	Spy	7/27	DUNN	Spy
2/2	STANFORD	Spy	8/3	MACDONNELL	Spy
2/9	DUNOUGHMORE	Spy	8/10	TERRY	Spy
2/16	BATTENBERG	Spy	8/17	MORLEY, S.H.	Spy
2/23	SEELY	Spy	8/24	ARNOLD-FORSTER	Spy
			8/31	LUCY *108	Spy
3/2	LAW, B.	Spy			
3/9	CASTLE	Spy	9/7	KUROPATKIN	Imp
3/16	MARCONI	Spy	9/14	BASS	Spy
3/23	TULLIBARDINE	Spy	9/21	BROCK	Spy
3/30	BROUGH	Spy	9/28	RIMINGTON-WILSON	Spy
4/6	CROOKS	Spy	10/5	HENRY	Spy
4/13	BALL	Spy	10/12	MARSHAM	Spy
4/20	ONSLOW	Spy	10/19	BOWLES *109	Spy
4/27	ELGIN	Spy	10/26	HOOD	Spy
5/4	MURRAY	Spy	11/2	TREVOR	Spy
5/11	GORDON	Spy	11/9	GUINNESS	Spy
5/18	CRITCHETT	Spy	11/16	GROSSMITH, W.	Spy
5/25	STEVENSON and		11/23	BROKE	Spy
	ROBERTS	Spy	11/30	FOOTE	Spy
6/1	WILLIAM (GERMAN		12/7	FOX-HUNTING	
	CROWN PRINCE)	Guth		CONSTELLATION	Bede
6/8	WALKER	Spy	12/14	ROBINSON	Spy
6/13	LAWRENCE	Spy	12/21	MENSDORFF	Spy
6/22	POYNDER	Spy	12/28	SHAW *110	Ruth
6/29	MINTO	Spy			

*Indicates subject is illustrated in Part I.

Date	Subject	Signed	Date	Subject	Signed
1/4	LUBBOCK	Bede	7/4	ROWE	Spy
1/11	GALLOWAY	Ruth	7/11	HAYWARD	Spy
1/18	BIRRELL	Spy	7/18	SPOONER	Spy
1/25	ROBSON	Spy	7/25	WEARDALE	Spy
2/1	PINERO *111	Bulbo	8/1	LEEDS	Spy
2/8	HARDIE	Spy	8/8	TYLDESLEY	Spy
2/15	GOUGH	Spy	8/15	GILLINGHAM	Spy
2/22	CECIL, R.	Spy	8/22	MAXWELL	Spy
			8/29	MATHERS	Spy
3/1	FITZWILLIAM	Spy	9/5	{ LODER	Spy
3/8	RIPON	Spy	9/5	{ GANT	Spy
3/15	BRASSEY	Spy	9/12	DILLON	Spy
3/22	LANE	Spy	9/19	LYTTON	Spy
3/29	BANKS	Spy	9/26	ST. ALBANS	Spy
4/5	PLYMOUTH	Spy			
4/12	BARLOW	Spy	10/3	CALLEY	Spy
4/19	STEPNEY	Spy	10/10	DOMVILE	Spy
4/26	TAYLOR	Spy	10/17	BRAY	Spy
			10/24	LOWTHER	Spy
5/3	THOMSON *112	Spy	10/31	McKENNA	Spy
5/10	McCALMONT	Spy			
5/17	WALDEN	Spy	11/7	TEMPLEMAN	Spy
5/24	ALFONSO XIII	Guth	11/14	HOCKING	Spy
5/31	EUGENIE of	Leslie	11/21	HIGGS	Spy
	BATTENBERG	Ward	11/28	GRIGGS	Spy
6/7	CAUSTON	Spy	12/5	HANBURY	Spy
6/14	FITZMAURICE	Spy	12/12	CORBET	Spy
6/21	WALKER	Spy	12/19	JOICEY	Spy
6/28	SCHUSTER	Spy	12/26	JELLICOE	Spy

*Indicates subject is illustrated in Part I.

Date	Subject	Signed	Date	Subject	Signed
1/2	BUXTON	Spy	7/3	JOHNSTONE	Spy
1/9	BUTLER, W.F.	Spy	7/10	WELLS	Spy
1/16	SMITH, F.E.	Spy	7/17	SUFFIELD	Ao
1/23	LEE	Spy	7/24	FOSTER	Spy
1/30	VAUGHAN	Spy	7/31	VANDERBILT	Spy
2/6	TRURO (STUBBS)	Spy	8/7	BULKELEY	Spy
2/13	ALTHORP	Spy	8/14	HUTCHINGS	Spy
2/20	REES	Spy	8/21	PORTSMOUTH	Spy
2/27	GILLETTE	Spy	8/28	THURSBY, J.	Spy
3/6	SOUTHAMPTON	Spy	9/4	BUCKMASTER	Spy
3/13	STUART	Spy	9/11	CARRINGTON	Spy
3/20	DE ROS	Spy	9/18	FRIPP	Spy
3/27	BIRON	Spy	9/25	AYLESFORD	Ao
4/3	BULL	Spy	10/2	SOVERAL	Ruth
4/10	RUSSELL	Spy	10/9	MacNAMARA	Spy
4/17	WOOD	Spy	10/16	LAURENCE	Spy
4/24	KEMBLE	Spy	10/23	LEA, H.C.	Spy
			10/30	FAY	Spy
5/1	O'CONOR	Spy			
5/8	DARLING	Spy	11/6	COLEMAN	Spy
5/15	O'BRIEN	Spy	11/13	GEORGE, D.L.	Spy
5/22	HERVEY	Ao	11/20	BUCHANAN	Spy
5/29	BOTHA	RYG	11/27	WARRINGTON	
6/5	MARTIN	Ao	12/4	LUCK	Spy
6/12	ROBERTSON	Spy	12/11	BUTLER, F.H.	Spy
6/19	PRENTICE	Spy	12/18	THURSBY, G.	Spy
6/26	BRAID	Spy	12/25	MAURIER	Spy

Date	Subject	Signed	Date	Subject	Signed
1/1	GILPIN	Spy	7/1	GRANARD	Spy
1/8	RAWLINSON	Spy	7/8	HALES	Spy
1/15	FORDHAM	Spy	7/15	PAGET, A.H.	Spy
1/22	MICHAELOVITCH	Spy	7/22	MAETERLINCK	Max
1/29	CHAMBERLAIN, J.	Who	7/29	WARD, J.	Spy
2/5	EDGCUMBE	Spy	8/5	ETHERINGTON-SMITH	Spy
2/12	EVANS	Spy	8/12	CRAWFORD	Spy
2/19	SAN GIULIANO	Spy	8/19	MacNAGHTEN	Spy
2/26	ELLIOTT	Spy	8/26	SHAUGHNESSY	Spy
3/4	ARMSTRONG	Spy	9/2	DEAKIN	Spy
3/11	INGLIS	Spy	9/9	BAILEY	Spy
3/18	HUNTLEY	Spy	9/16	WINTERTON	Spy
3/25	REDWOOD	Spy	9/23	BRIGHT, C.	Spy
			9/30	BIRD	Spy
4/1	BURY	Spy			
4/8	MACKIE	Spy	10/7	JAURES	Guth
4/15	SAVILE	Spy	10/14	NEWTON	Spy
4/22	JARDINE	Spy	10/21	FURNESS	Spy
4/29	HAMBOURG	Spy	10/28	RICHARDSON	Who
5/6	WRIGHTSON	Spy	11/4	TRUSCOTT	Spy
5/13	CLEMENS *114	Spy	11/11	GRANET	Spy
5/20	AYNESWORTH	Spy	11/18	{ BOURGES	Guth
5/27	CLEMENCEAU	Vanitas		{ LADY NEVILL	Who
			11/25	BURTON	Spy
6/3	COOPER	Spy			
6/10	MASON	Max	12/2	RAMSAY	Spy
6/17	SALOMONS	Spy	12/9	ALEXANDER of TECK	Spy
6/24	CURZON	Spy	12/16	PLOWDER	Spy
			12/23	DE LARA	
			12/30	NELKE	Elf

*Indicates subject is illustrated in Part I.

Date	Subject	Signed	Date	Subject	Signed
1/6	WILBERFORCE	Spy	8/4	LEITH	Spy
1/13	COLERIDGE	Spy	8/11	ANATOLE FRANCE	Guth
1/20	ALEXANDER	Max	8/18	KINCAID-SMITH	Spy
1/27	CHESTERFIELD	Spy	8/25	CAMPBELL	Spy
2/3	ROBINSON	Spy	9/1	COX	Kite
2/10	SHUTTLEWORTH	Spy	9/8	WOOTON	Spy
2/17	REGNART	Spy		"MINORU"	Percy Earl
2/24	SARGENT	Max	9/15	WASON	Who
				"BAYARDO"	Percy Earl
3/3	KEPPEL	Spy	9/22	BLATHWAYT	Spy
3/10	HORLICK	Spy		"CYLLENE"	Percy Earl
3/17	MEYER	Spy	9/29	JACKSON	Spy
3/24	BENSON	Sho		"DEAN SWIFT"	Percy Earl
3/31	FRY	Spy			
			10/6	SHACKLETON	Kite
4/7	MALLABY-DEELEY	Spy		LUNN	Elf
4/14	SCOTT	Who	10/13	WALKER, E.D.	Quip
4/21	INVERCLYDE	Spy		"LUTTEUR III"	Emil Adam
4/28	BARRINGTON	Spy	10/20	JARDINE	Elf
				"SCEPTRE" and "MAID	
5/5	NEWLANDS	Spy		OF CORINTH"	Percy Earl
5/12	WALKER, J.R.	Spy	10/27	BRETTON	Spy
5/19	HEMMERDE	Spy		"PRETTY POLLY"	Percy Earl
5/26	FITZGERALD	Spy			
			11/3	FIELDING	Who
6/2	LUCAS	Elf		"ST. SIMON"	Percy Earl
6/9	WINANS	Who	11/10	MONOEL OF	
6/16	TATLOW	Spy		PORTUGAL	NIBS
6/23	PARKER	Spy	11/17	BOSWORTH	Elf
6/30	CURNICK	Spy		"ROCK SAND"	Percy Earl
			11/24	FRISWELL	HCO
7/7	REUTER	Spy		"PERSIMMON"*113	Percy Earl
7/14	COURTENAY	Spy			
7/21	SINCLAIR	Spy	12/1	WILLIAMS, A.O.	HCO
7/28	PALMER	Elf		"FLYING FOX"	Percy Earl
			12/8	BARKER	Elf
			12/16	WILLIAMSON, A.	HCO
			12/23	TENNANT, H.J.	Spy
				CARLILE	Elf
			12/30	HARRIS	Spy
				VICKERS	Spy

*Indicates subject is illustrated in Part I.

Date	Subject	Signed	Date	Subject	Signed
1/6	YOUNGER	Pip	7/6	FORSTER	Elf
	BARKER	HCO	7/13	CRICHTON-STUART	Who
	BELILIOS		7/20	VASSER-SMITH	HCO
	DU CROS	HCO	7/27	COLERIDGE	Elf
1/13	BAKER	Elf			
1/20	JOEL	HCO	8/3	BLYTHE	Als
1/27	BALFOUR	Xit	8/10	DENNY	Who
	"SANTRY"	Frank Patton	8/17	HUNTINGTON, W.B.	Pry
			8/24	KING	HCO
2/3	SUTTON	Elf	8/31	BARRYMORE	Spy
2/10	RUGGLES-BRISE	Spy			
	"TORPOINT"	Percy Earl	9/7	BUCHANAN	Quip
2/17	TWINING	HCO	9/14	STEPHENS	Elf
2/24	HENNESSEY	HCO	9/21	BARING	Spy
			9/28	SIMPSON	Spy
3/3	LYONS	HCO			
3/10	WELBY	HCO	10/5	RENAN	Guth
3/17	ASQUITH	Xit	10/12	RIDLEY	Who
3/24	WIPPELL	Elf	10/19	EMMOTT	Who
3/31	WORKMAN	Elf	10/26	HERSCHELL	Who
4/7	WATTS	Spy	11/2	TENNANT	Who
4/14	BUTE	Who	11/9	GARCKE	HLO
4/21	BRINCKMAN	Elf		GLANTAWE	Who
4/28	YERBURGH	Who	11/16	COLLAPSE OF THE	
				CONFERENCE	Mouse
5/5	DREXEL	Elf	11/23	HOZ	Who
5/12	EDWARD VII	Xit	11/30	WATERLOW	Who
5/19	NUTTING	Pry			
5/26	HUNTINGTON, C.P.	Quip	12/7	AINSWORTH	Who
			12/14	CHETWODE	Who
6/1	PORTER	Xit	12/21	BUTT	HCO
6/8	TURNER	Who	12/29	COLLINS	Wallace Hester
6/15	PANKHURST	Spy			
6/22	OWEN	Elf			
6/29	COX	Spy			

Date	Subject	Signed	Date	Subject	Signed
1/4	STOLL	Ape,Jr.	7/5	MATCHAM	Nibs
1/11	RAVENSCROFT	Ape,Jr.	7/12	PRINCE of WALES	Nibs
1/18	LUSH	Ape,Jr.	7/19	CRAIG	Who
1/25	ELLISON	Hester	7/26	KEKEWICH	Who
2/1	FOY	HCO	8/2	COCHRANE	Spy
2/8	CARSON	Hester	8/9	SMITH, F.E.	Nibs
2/15	DRISCOLL	Ape,Jr.	8/16	SHAW	Ritchie
2/22	ROBERTS	Spy	8/23	ELLENBOROUGH	Who
			8/30	CROMPTON	Who
3/1	COLLINS	Ape,Jr.			
3/8	CHURCHILL	Nibs	9/6	HOLCROFT	HLO
3/15	EVE	Ape,Jr.	9/13	GARVIN	Ritchie
3/22	ORDE	Ape,Jr.	9/20	NOTT-BOWER	Ray
3/29	BOURNE	Ape,Jr.	9/27	GOULD	Wh—
4/5	TREE	Nibs	10/4	ALLINSON	Ray
4/12	SHEPPARD	Ape,Jr.	10/11	TALBOT	Ray
4/19	BADEN-POWELL	Ape,Jr.	10/18	SIMON	Wh—
4/26	EDWARDS	Nibs	10/25	ASKWITH	Wh—
5/3	HUTCHINSON	Ape,Jr.	11/1	CODY	Ritchie
5/10	GRAHAME-WHITE	Tec	11/8	CROSBY	Wh
5/17	PYKE	Ape,Jr.	11/15	HAMMERSTEIN	Ray
5/24	ROBINSON	Spy	11/22	BETTINSON	Wh
5/31	ELPHINSTONE	Ape,Jr.	11/29	ASCHE	Ritchie
6/7	QUEEN ALEXANDRA }	Sig. Unclear	12/6	SELFRIDGE	Ritchie
6/14	HOUSTON	Spy	12/13	McAULIFFE	Ritchie
6/21 {	BROWN	Spy	12/20	WOLF	Ritchie
	GEORGE V	Ape,Jr.	12/27	WILSON	Ritchie
6/28	SCRUTTON	Ape,Jr.			

Date	Subject	Signed	Date	Subject	Signed
1/3	FISHER	Ray	7/3	CARTER	Wh
1/10	LORAINE	Ritchie	7/10	CROSSE	Wh
1/17	CARSON	Wh	7/17	CHEYLESMORE	Wh
1/24	JONES	Wh	7/24	SWINTON	Ray
1/31	INGE	Wh	7/31	HAMEL	Wh
2/7	SAVAGE	Ray	8/7	HOBBS	Wh
2/14	CORRI	Ritchie	8/14	GRIFFITH-BOSCAWEN	Ray
2/21	CHESTERTON	Strickland	8/21	HASSALL	Strickland
2/28	SHUSTER	Wh	8/28	JERNINGHAM	Wh
3/6	LANE	Strickland	9/4	HADFIELD	Wh
3/13	MACARA	Ritchie	9/11	KINNARD	Wh
3/20	CRADOCK-HARTOPP	Wh	9/18	BROOKS	Wh
3/27	RYLE	Wh	9/25	TATE	Wh
4/3	SWANN	Wh	10/2	CAMBON	K
4/10	LAW	Strickland	10/9	WALDEGRAVE	Wh
4/17	MASCAGNI	Wh	10/16	LEE	K
4/24	HENSON	Wh	10/23	LASCELLES	K
			10/30	BERNHARDT	K
5/1	FORD	Strickland			
5/8	SPICER	Ray	11/6	LADY NEVILL	K
5/15	OSBORN	Wh	11/13	SOVERAL	K
5/22	INGRAM	Wh	11/20	WEST	K
5/29	COOP	Wh	11/27	ANNALY	K
6/5	REE	Wh	12/4	DENISON	Wh
6/12	HOLLEBONE	Wh	12/11	WELLINGTON	Wh
6/19	LONSDALE	Wh	12/18	IRVING	Wh
6/26	SYKES	Wh	12/25	HALL-WALKER	Wh

Date	Subject	Signed	Date	Subject	Signed
1/1	BROWNLOW	WH	7/2	GORE	Cock
1/8	INGLIS	WH	7/9	JOHNSTONE	Hester
1/15	ALVERSTONE	WH	7/16	CONNAUGHT	Hester
1/22	BURR	WH	7/23	HALBRONN	Owl
1/29	KNOX	WH	7/30	TUPPER	Owl
2/5	WOOD	Hester	8/6	ALLOM	Owl
2/12	(NONE PUBLISHED IN		8/13	NICHOLSON	Owl
	THIS ISSUE)		8/20	LE SAGE	Owl
2/19	SCOTT	Hester	8/27	BEBEL	
2/26	EADIE	W.Hester			
			9/3	DILLON, E.W.	Owl
3/5	HEWLETT	W.Hester	9/10	TELLEGEN	Owl
3/12	WILSON *115	W.Hester	9/17	RANKIN	Owl
3/19	HALDANE	Owl	9/24	REID	Owl
3/26	GREY	Owl			
			10/1	DICK	Ast
4/2	BENNETT	Owl	10/8	STOLL	Owl
4/9	HUMPHREY	Wallace Hester	10/15	CONNAUGHT	Owl
4/16	BANBURY	Eianley Cock	10/22	STEVENS	Ast
4/23	McKENNA	Owl	10/29	RHYS-WILLIAMS	Owl
4/30	BROOKFIELD	Ritchie			
			11/5	DILLON	Owl
5/7	LAVERY	Ritchie	11/12	HARRIS	Owl
5/14	ESMOND	Hester	11/19	BUCKMASTER	Owl
5/21	LANE	Cock	11/26	SAVAGE-LANDOR	Ast
5/28	NIKISCH	Owl			
			12/3	RONALD	Ast
6/4	FORBES-ROBERTSON	Ritchie	12/10	ROZE	Ast
6/11	PHILLPOTTS	Ritchie	12/17	FOSS	Ast
6/18	ISAACS	Owl	12/24	FOOTE	Ast
6/25	POINCARE	Owl	12/31	PLYMOUTH	Hic

*Indicates subject is illustrated in Part I.

1914

The first three issues for this year contained drawings (Joseph Chamberlain by "Ast"; Charles Urban by "Spy"; and Charles Wyndham by "Ast"). The January 14 issue carried an "IMPORTANT" notice that the proprietors of the "London Budget" had acquired both *Vanity Fair* and a women's magazine, *Hearth and Home*. The January 21 issue noted that preparations were underway for a merger of the two magazines into "a high-class ladies weekly." With this issue, the caricatures abruptly ceased appearing, and, on February 5, 1914, the new magazine made its debut under the title *Vanity Fair & Hearth & Home*. The only retained resemblance to the original *Vanity Fair* was its name in the shared title. The new magazine continued until 1929.

PART III

SUBJECT INDEX

Cairns, Lord, 69
Calcraft, Mr. Henry G., 80
Calley, Colonel, 106
Calthorp, Lord, 85
Calvert, Alfred Frederick, 95
Cambon, M. Pierre Paul, 99,112
Cambridge, H.R.H., The Duke of, 70
Cameron, Lieutenant, 76
Campbell, Sir George, 78
Campbell, The Rt. Hon. James,109
Campbell, John (see Argyll)
Campbell and Stratheden, Lord, 73
Campbell, The Rev. R. J., 104
Campbell-Bannerman, The Right Hon. Sir Henry, 99
Camperdown, The Earl of, 95
Canning, Hubert (see Clanricarde)
Cannon, H. Mornington, 91
Cannon, Tom, 85
Canterbury, The Archbishop of, 69
Capel, Monsignor Thos. J., 72
Carden, Alderman Sir Robert, 80
Cardross, Lord, 84
Cardwell, Rt. Hon. Edward, 69
Carington, Col. The Hon. W.H.P., 93
Carleton, Dudley (see Dorchester)
Carlile, Colonel E. Hildred, 109
Carlos VII (Carlos Raphael,Pretender to Spanish Throne),76
Carlyle, Thomas, 70
Carmarthen, Marquis of, 89
Carnarvon, Lord, 69
Carnegie, Mr. Andrew, 103
Carnot, M. Marie Francois Sadi, 89
Carpenter, Wm. (see Bishop Ripon)
Carr, Mr. J. E. Comyns, 93
Carrington, Lord, 74, 107
Carson, Ed. H., 93, 111
Carson, The Rt. Hon Sir E., 112
Carte, Mr. Richard D'Oyly, 91
Carter, Mr. John Corrie, 112
Carter, Mr. Robert Brudenell,92
Cartwright, Mr. William Cornwallis, 84
Casimir-Perier, M. Pierre Paul,94
Cassagnac, Mr. Paul De Granier De, 79
Cassel, Sir Ernest, 99
Castle, Mr. Egerton, 105
Castlereagh, Viscount, 79

Catena, The Count Della, 93
Cathcart, The Earl, 88
Causton, The Rt. Hon. R.K. 106
Cave, The Hon. Sir L.W., 93
Cave, The Rt. Hon Stephen, 74
Cavendish, Chas. (see Chesham)
Cavendish, Lord Edward, 86
Cavendish, Mr. Richard Frederick, 100
Cavendish, Spencer (see Devonshire)
Cavendish, Spender-Cavendish (see Hartington)
Cavendish, Mr. Victor, M.P., 95
Cayzer, Sir Charles W., 104
Cecil, Mr. Arthur, 89
Cecil, Lord Edward Herbert, 99
Cecil, Lord Hugh, 100
Cecil, Hugh (see Lonsdale)
Cecil, Lord Robert, 106
Cetewayo, King of Zululand, 82
Chamberlain, Mr. Austen, 99
Chamberlain, Joseph, 77,101,108, 114
Chambers, Sir Thomas, 84
Chandos-Pole, Mr. Reginald, 88
Chang, Li Hung, 96
Chang, Ta-Jen, 103
Channel, Mr. Justice A.M., 98
Channing, Chas. (see Dungarvan)
Chaplin, Mr. Henry, 74
Chapman, Captain Wilfrid Hubert (President of C.U.B.C.), 103
Charles, The Rt. Hon. Sir Arthur, 88
Charles, H.R.H. Prince of Denmark, 102
Chelmsford, General Lord, 81
Chelmsford, Lord, 70
Chenery, Mr. Thomas, 79
Chesham, The Lord, 100
Chesterfield, The Earl of, 109
Chesterton, Mr. G. K., 112
Chetwode, Col. Sir P.W., 110
Chetwynd, Sir George, 85
Chetwynd-Talbot, Chas. (see Shrewsbury/Talbot)
Chevalier, M. Michel, 75
Cheylesmore, The Lord, 112
Childers, Right Hon. H.C.E., 69
Chitty, The Hon. Sir Joseph William, 85
Choate, J.H. The American Ambassador, 99

Edward VII, His Majesty King,
78,102,110
Edwardes, Mr. George, 111
Edwards, Mr. H., 82
Edwards, Mr. John Passmore, 85
Egerton, Major E.H., 89
Egerton of Tatton, Lord, 86
Egerton, Thomas (see Ellesmere)
Eglinton and Winton, The Earl
of, 96
Eiffel, M. Alexandre Gustave, 89
Elcho, Lord, 70,92
Elgin, The Earl of, 105
Elizabeth, H.I.M. The Empress
of Austria, 84
Ellenborough, The Lord, 86,111
Ellesmere, The Earl of, 87
Ellice, General Sir Charles
Henry, 77
Ellicott, The Rt. Rev. Charles
John, Bishop of Gloucester
& Bristol, 85
Elliot, Sir George, Bart., 79
Elliot, The Right Hon. Sir
Henry George, 77
Elliott, Mr. George, 108
Ellis, Sir John Whitaker, Lord
Mayor of London, 82
Ellis, Mr. Robinson, 94
Ellison, Hon. Price, 111
Ellison-Macartney, Mr. W.G., 93
Elphinstone, Lord, 111
Elphinstone, Sir James Dalrymple
Horn, 78
Elton, Mr. Charles Isaac, 87
Emmott, The Rt. Hon. A., 110
Enfield, Viscount, 72
Errington, Mr. George, 82
Erskine, Mr. Henry David, 94
Escott, Mr. T.H.S., 85
Eslington, Lord, 76
Esmond, Henry V., 113
Esterhazy, Major, 98
Etherington-Smith, Mr.
Raymond Broadley, 108
Eugenie, H.R.H. Victoria, of
Battenberg (Queen of Spain),
106
Eustace-Jameson, Major, 104
Evans, Sir Francis H., 96
Evans, Sir Samuel Thomas, 108
Evans-Gordon, Major, 105
Eve, Mr. Justice, 111
Ewart, Colonel Henry P., 81

Exeter, The Marquis of, 81
Eykyn, Mr. Roger, 72
Eyton, Cannon Robt., 98

F

Faber, Mr. George Denison, 100
Falmouth, Viscount, 77,98
Farquhar, Lord, 98
Farquharson of Invercauld,
Colonel James, 76
Farquharson, Dr. Robert, 95
Farrar, The Venerable Frederick
William, 91
Farwell, Mr. Justice Geo., 100
Faure, M. Francois Felix,
President of the French
Republic, 95
Fawcett, Mr. Henry, 72
Fay, Mr. Sam, 107
Fellowes, The Hon. Ailwyn, 96
Fenton, Sir Myles, 90
Fergusson, Sir James, 92
Fergusson, Mr. Samuel Mure, 93
Fergusson, Sir William, 70
Feversham, The Earl of, 78
Field, Rear-Admiral Edward, 91
Field, Mr. Justice Wm. V., 87
Fielding, The Hon. W.S., 109
Fielding, William (see Denbigh)
Fife, The Earl of, 89
Fildes, Mr. Luke, 92
Findlay, Sir George, 92
Finlay, Mr. Robert Bannatyne, 88
Firr, Thomas, 84
Fish, Hon. Hamilton, American
Secretary of State for Foreign
Affairs, 72
Fisher, Vice-Admiral Sir
Frederic W., 112
Fisher, Admiral Sir John
Arbuthnot, 102
Fisher, Mr. William Hayes, 100
Fitzalan-Howard, Henry (see
Norfolk)
Fitz Gerald, Lord Gerald, 83
Fitzgerald, Maurice, The Knight
of Kerry, 101,109
Fitzgerald, The Rt. Hon. Lord
Otho Augustus, 73
Fitzgerald, The Rt. Hon. Sir Wm.
Robert Robert Seymour Vesey,74
Fitzherbert, Mr. W., 96
Fitzmaurice, Lord, 106
Fitzmaurice, Lord Edmond George,78

125

Gerard, Lord, 78
Gervais, Admiral, 102
Gilbey, Mr. Walter, 88
Gibson, The Rt. Hon. Edward, 85
Giers, Monsieur De, 84
Giffard, Sir Hardinge Stanley, 78
Gifford, H.S. (see Halsbury)
Gifford, Captain Lord, V.C., 80
Gilbert, William S., 81
Gill, Mr. Charles Frederick, 91
Gillette, Mr. William, 107
Gillingham, The Rev. F.H.,106
Gilpin, Mr. Charles, 73
Gilpin, Mr. Peter Purcell, 108
Gladstone, Mr. Herbert John, 82
Gladstone, Prof. John Hall, 91
Gladstone, Wm. Ewart, 69,79,80,
    81,87
Gladstone, Mr. William Henry,82
Glantawe, Lord, 110
Gleichen, Count Albert Edward
    Wilfrid, 98
Gleichen, Vice-Admiral
    H.S.H. Count, 84
Glyn, Hon. George Grenfell, 72
Godfrey, Lieutenant and
    Bandmaster Daniel, 88
Gold, Mr. Harcourt Gilbey, 99
Goldmann, Mr. Charles Sydney,
    104
Goldney, Mr. Gabriel, 72
Goldsmid, Sir Francis Henry, 72
Goldsmid, Sir Julian, 87
Gomm, Field-Marshall Sir
    William, 73
Gooch, Captain Arthur, 82
Gooch, Sir Daniel, 82
Goodford, The Rev. Charles Old,
    (*Old Goody*), 76
Goodwin, The Rt. Rev. Harvey,
    Bishop of Carlisle, 88
Gordon, Lieut.-Colonel Charles
    George, 81
Gordon, The Rt. Hon. E.
    Strathearn, 74
Gordon, J.C. (see Aberdeen)
Gordon-Cumming, Sir William
    Alexander, 80
Gordon-Lennox, Lord Henry
    G.C., 70
Gordon-Lennox, Lord Walter
    Charles, 92
Gore, A.W., 113
Gorst, Mr. John Eldon, 80

Goschen, Right Hon. G.J., 69
Gossett, Captain Ralph Allen, 74
Gough, General Sir Hugh, 106
Gould, Sir A. Pearce, 111
Gould, Mr. Francis Carruthers, 90
Gould, Mr. George Jay, 94
Gounod, Mr. Francois, 79
Gouraud, Col. Geo. E., 89
Grace, Mr. William Gilbert, 77
Gradock-Hartopp, Sir Chas., 112
Grafton, Major-General The
    Duke of, 86
Graham, Douglas (see Montrose)
Graham, Mr. H.R., 93
Grahame-White, Mr. Claude, 111
Grain, Mr. Corney, 85
Granard, The Earl of, 108
Granet, Mr. W. Guy, 108
Grant, Mr. Albert, 74
Grant, Sir Francis, 71
Grant, General Ulysses S.,
    President of the United States
    of America, 72
Grant-Duff, Mr. M.E., 69
Grantham, Sir William, 90
Granville, Earl, 69
Greeley, Mr. Horace, Candidate
    for the Presidency, 72
Green, Mr. Joseph Fletcher, 90
Greenall, Sir Gilbert, 99
Greenwell, Mr. Walpole, 98
Greenwood, Mr. Frederick, 80
Gregory, Mr. George Burrow, 80
Gregory, M. William Henry, 71
Grenfell, Major-General Sir
    Francis, 89
Grenfell, Mr. William Henry, 90
Greville, The Hon. Sidney
    Robert, 100
Grevy, M. Jules, 79
Grey, Earl, 69, 98
Grey, The Earl De, 90
Grey, Sir Edward, 103
Grey, Sir Edward, 113
Grieve, Mr. John Mackenzie, 77
Griffith-Boscawen, Sir A.S.T., 112
Griggs, William, 106
Grimthrope, The Rt. Hon. Lord, 89
Grossmith, Mr. George, 88
Grossmith, Mr. Weedon, 105

Groups (Listed chronologically by caption. Selected subjects from
   each are noted.)

A ROW IN THE SEASON, 79 (English Society at Hyde Park)
THE FOURTH PARTY, 80 (R. Churchill, H.D. Wolff, Gorst)
TREASURY BENCH, 80 (Gladstone, Hartington, Chamberlain)
BIRTH, BEHAVIOR AND BUSINESS, 81 (Northcote, Manner, Cross)
FORCE NO REMEDY, 81 (Parnell)
PURSE, PUSSY, PIETY, 82 (Northbrook, Granville, Selborne,
   Salisbury)
CABINET COUNCIL, 83 (Gladstone, Chamberlain, Harcourt,
   and others)
NEWMARKET, 85
LOBBY OF HOUSE OF COMMONS, 86 (Bright, Harcourt, Chamberlain,
   Parnell, Gladstone, and others)
TATTERSALL'S, 87 (Prince of Wales and numerous others)
WINNING POST, 88 (Watts, Rickaby, and six other jockeys)
IN VANITY FAIR, 90 (Twenty-two figures, including "Spy")
BENCH AND BAR, 91 (Several Justices and Judges)
MIXED POLITICAL WARES, 92 (Gladstone, Harcourt, Spencer,
   Ripon, Campbell-Bannerman, and Fowler)
ON THE TERRACE, 93 (Balfour, Chamberlain, Gorst, Temple,
   Harcourt, Mundella, and McCarthy)
AT COWES, 94 (Prince of Wales and other distinguished
   yachtsmen)
A MASTERS' MEET, 95 (Lords Lonsdale and Portman and
   several other fox-hunters)
ON THE HEATH, 96 (John Porter and other Turf Enthusiasts)
CYCLING IN HYDE PARK, 96 (Lady Nevill and other Lady
   Cyclers)
EMPIRE MAKERS AND BREAKERS, 97 (Cecil Rhodes and others)
AU BOIS DE BOULOGNE, 97 (Princess de Sagan and other
   leaders of Parisian Society)
LORD PROTECT US!, 98 (Balfour, Chamberlain, and others)
AT RENNES, 99 (Dreyfus in Court Scene)
A GENERAL GROUP, 100 (Roberts, Kitchner, and other
   Military Leaders)
KIRBY GATE, 101 (Mrs. Asquith and other male and female
   Fox Hunters)
HEADS OF THE LAW, 102 (Chief Justice Alverstone and nine
   other Justices)
A FOX-HUNTING CONSTELLATION, 105 (Prominent English Huntsmen
   at the Belvoir Hunt)
COLLAPSE OF THE CONFERENCE, 110

128

Grove, Sir George, 91
Grove, Sir William Robert, 87
Guest, Mr. Arthur Edward, 96
Guest, Mr. Montague John, 80
Guest, Mr. Thomas Merthy, 97
Guinness, Hon. Rupert, 105
Gull, Sir William Withey, 75
Gully, Mr. James Manby, 76
Gully, The Speaker William, 96
Gurdon, Mr. Edward Temple, 92
Gurney, The Rt. Hon. Russell, 71

H

Haag, Mr. Carl, 84
Hadfield, Sir Robert, 112
Haggard, Mr. Henry Rider, 87
Haig, Mr. Neil, 98
Haines, General Sir Frederick
    Paul, 76
Halbronn, M. Cheri R., 113
Haldane, Mr. R. Burdon, 96
Haldane, Lord, 113
Haldon, Lord (Lawrence Palk), 84
Haldon, Lord ("Piggy" Palk), 82
Hale, The Rev. Edward, 92
Hales, Mr. A.G., 108
Halifax, Lord (Sir Chas. Wood),
    70
Hall, Mr. Charles, 88
Hall, Mr. Edward Marshall, 103
Hall, General Julian Hamilton,
    98
Hall, Rev. Newman, 72
Hall-Walker, Col. William, 112
Halsbury, Lord, 90
Hambourg, Mr. Mark, 108
Hamel, Mr. Gustav, 112
Hamilton, The Rt. Hon. Lord
    Claud, 77
Hamilton, Lord Claud John, 78
Hamilton, The Rt. Hon. Lord
    George Francis, 79
Hamilton, General Sir Ian
    Standish Monteith Hamilton,
    101
Hamilton, Lord Frederic Spencer,
    95
Hamilton, The Marquis of, 81,99
Hamilton, William Alexander
    Louis Stephen Hamilton-
    Douglas, Duke of, 73
Hamley, Lieut.-General Sir
    Edward Bruce, 87
Hammerstein, Mr. Oscar, 111

Hammond, Lord, 75
Hamond, Mr. C.F., 93
Hanbury, Mr. Evan, 106
Hanbury, Tracy, The Hon.
    Frederick Stephen Archibald,84
Hanbury, The Rt. Hon. Robert
    William, 96
Hannay, Mr. James Lennox, 98
Hannen, The Rt. Hon. Sir James,88
Hanotaux, M. Gabriel, 96
Hansard, Mr. Henry, 84
Hanson, Sir Reginald (The Rt.
    Hon. The Lord Mayor of
    London), 86
Harcourt, Mr. Lewis Vernon, 95
Harcourt, Sir William George
    Granville Venables Vernon, 99
Hardie, Mr. J. Keir, 106
Hardwicke, The Earl of, 101
Hardwicke, Lord (C.P.Yorke), 74
Hardy, Rt. Hon. Gathorne, 72
Hardy, Mr. Thomas, 92
Hare, Mr. John, 90
Hargreaves, Col. John, 87
Hargreaves, Mr. John, 99
Harmsworth, Mr. Alfred Charles, 95
Harrington, The Earl of, 73,91
Harris, Mr. Augustus Henry
    Glossop, 89
Harris, Frank, 113
Harris, Mr. Frederick Leverton,
    109
Harris, Lord, 81
Harrison, The Venerable Benjamin,
    85
Harrison, Mr. Frederic, 86
Harrison, Mr. Frederick, 94
Harrowby, The Earl of, 71,85
Hart, Sir Robert, 94
Harte, Mr. Francis Bret, 79
Hartington, The Marquis of, 69,88
Hassall, Mr. John, 112
Hastie, Mr. A.H., 93
Hastings, The Rt. Hon. Lord, 86
Hatherley, Lord, 69
Hatherton, Lord (Ed.Littleton),95
Havelock, Major-General Sir
    Henry Marshann, 79
Havilland, Mr. Reginald Saumarez
    De, 101
Hawarden, Viscount, 81
Haweis, The Rev. Hugh Reginald,88
Hawke, Lord, 92
Hawkins, Mr. Anthony Hope, 95

Hawkins, Mr. Henry, 73
Hawley, Sir Joseph, 70
Hawtrey, Mr. Charles, 92
Hay, Rear-Admiral Lord John, 75
Hay, The Rt. Hon. Sir John
    Charles Dalrymple, 75
Hay, Mr. John, The United States
    Ambassador, 97
Hay, Lord William, 74
Hay, William Montagu (see
    Tweeddale)
Hayashi, The Viscount Tadasu, 102
Hayward, Mr. Abraham, 75
Hayward, Thomas, 106
Headfort, The Marquess of, 77
Headlam, The Rt. Hon. Thomas
    Emerson, 73
Headley, Lord, 80
Healy, Mr. Timothy Michael, 86
Heaton, Mr. John Henniker, 87
Helder, Mr. August, 96
Helps, Sir Arthur, 74
Hely-Hutchinson, The Hon. Sir
    Walter Francis, 98
Hemmerde, Mr. Edward G., 109
Hemphill, Mr. Charles Hare, 104
Henderson, Lieutenant-Colonel
    Edmund Yeamans Wallcott, 75
Heneage, Admiral Sir Algernon
    Charles Fieschi, 101
Heneage, The Rt. Hon. Edward, 87
Henley, The Rt. Hon. Joseph
    Warner, 74
Henley, Mr. W.E., 92
Hennessey, Mr. James Richard, 110
Hennessy, His Excellency Governor
    John Pope-, 75
Henniker, Lord, 82
Henry, Mr. Edward Richard, 105
Henry, Mr. Mitchell, 79
Henry, Prince of Orleans, 97
Henson, The Rev. H. Hensley, 112
Herbert, Sir Michael Henry, 103
Herbert of Muckross, Mr.
    Henry Arthur, 76
Herbert, The Hon. Sidney, 86
Herkomer, Mr. Hubert, 84
Hermon-Hodge, Mr. Robert
    Trotter, 92
Herschell, Sir Farrer, 81
Herschell, Lord, 110
Hertford, The Marquess of, 77
Hervey, The Rev. Canon, 107
Hessey, The Rev. James, 74

Hewlett, Maurice H., 113
Hibbert, Mr. Washington, 73
Higginson, Lieutenant-General
    George Wentworth, Alexander, 84
Higgs, William, 106
Higgins, Mr. Henry Vincent, 98
Hiley-Hoskins, Rear-Admiral Sir
    Anthony, 83
Hill, Lord Arthur William, 86
Hill, Mr. G. Rowland, 90
Hillier, William (see Onslow)
Hilton, Mr. Horace Harold, 103
Hirsch, Baron, 90
Hirst, George, 103
Hoare, Sir Henry Ainslie, 83
Hobart Pasha, Admiral, 78
Hobbs, Mr. T. Berry, 112
Hocking, Mr. Silas Kitto, 106
Hogg, Colonel James MacNaghten, 73
Holcroft, Sir Chas., 111
Hole, Dean, 95
Holford, Captain George Lindsay,
    99
Holker, Sir John, 78
Holland, The Rt. Hon. Sir Henry
    Thurstan, 87
Hollman, Mr. Joseph, 97
Holland, The Lady, 84
Holland, Hon. Sydney, 104
Hollebone, Mr. R.A. Stewart, 112
Holmes, Dr. Oliver Wendell, 86
Holms, John, 82
Hood, Sir Alexander Fuller-
    Acland, 103
Hood, Hon. A. Nelson, 105
Hooley, Mr. Ernest Terah, 96
Hope, John (see Hopetoun)
Hopetoun, The Earl of, 100
Horlick, Mr. James, J.F., 109
Hornby, Mr. Albert Neilson, 91
Hornby, Mr. J. J., The Provost
    of Eton, 101
Horsford, Lieut.-General Sir
    Alfred Hastings, 77
Horsman, Rt. Hon. Edward, 72
Houghton, Lord (R.M. Milnes), 70
Houghton, The Rt. Hon. Lord, 92
Houldsworth, Mr. J.H., 90
Houldsworth, Mr. William Henry, 85
Houston, Mr. R.P., 111
Hothfield, The Rt. Hon. Lord, 89
Howard (see Suffolk and Berkshire)
Howard, the Hon. Kenneth, 92
Howard, Mr. Morgan, 81

L

Labouchere, Mr. Henry Du Pre, 74
Lagden, Sir Godfrey Yeatman, 101
Laing, Mr. Samuel, 73
Laird, Mr. John, 73
Laking, Sir Francis Henry, 103
Lalaing, Count Charles De, 104
Lambton (see Durham)
Lambton, The Hon. George, 104
Lambton, Captain the Hon.
   Hedworth, 100
Lamington, Lord, 92
Lane, Mr. Norman Angell, 112
Lane, W. Arbuthnot, 113
Lane, Major-General Sir R.B., 106
Lane-Fox, of Bramham, George,78
Lang, C.G. (see Bishop Stepney)
Lankester, Professor Ray, 105
Lansdowne, The Marquis of, 74
Lara, Mr. Isidore De, 108
Larking, Colonel Cuthbert, 88
Lascelles, Sir Frank, 112
Lascelles, Sir Frank Cavendish,
   102
Lascelles, The Hon. Gerald
   William, 97
Laurier, The Rt. Hon. Sir
   Wilfred, 97
Lavery, Mr. John, 113
Law, Mr. A. Bonar, 112
Law, Mr. Bonar, 105
Law, Chas. Edmund (see
   Ellenborough)
Lawes, Mr. Charles Bennet, 83
Lawes, Sir John Bennet, 82
Lawley, Beilby (see Wenlock)
Lawrence, Mr. Justice A.T., 107
Lawrence, Mr. Justice J.C., 97
Lawrence, Sir James John Trevor,
   99
Lawrence, Lord John, 71
Lawrence, Sir Walter T., 105
Lawson, Mr. H.L.W., 93
Lawson, Mr. Lionel, 76
Lawson, Sir Wilfrid, 72
Layard, Rt. Hon. A.H., 69
Lea, Mr. Hugh Cecil, 107
Leach, Lieutenant-Colonel Sir
   George, 96
Lechmere, Sir Edmund Anthony
   Harley, 83
Lecky, Mr. William Edward
   Hartpoll, 82
Lee, Mr. Arthur Hamilton, 107
Lee, Sir Henry Austin, 112

Leeds, The Duke of, 106
Leeman, Mr. George, 72
Leeson, E.N. (see Milltown)
Lefevre, Sir John George Shaw-, 71
Legard, The Rev. Cecil, 101
Legge, Augustus (see Lichfield)
Leicester, The Earl of, 83
Leigh, Mr. E.C. Austen, 101
Leighton, Mr. Frederick, 72
Leith, Mr. John Farley, 79
Leith, Lord of Fyvie, 109
Lehmann, Mr. Rudolf Chambers, 95
Leng, Sir William Christopher,90
Leo XIII, His Holiness Pope, 78
Leopold, H.R.H. Prince, 77
Leopold II, King of the Belgians,
   69
Le Sage, J.M., 113
Leslie-Melville, Alexander (see
   Leven and Melville)
Lessar, M. Paul, 85
Lesseps, Le Vicomte Ferdinand De,
   69
Letchworth, Sir Edward, 103
Leven and Melville, The Earl of,
   81
Leveson-Gower, Mr. George
   Granville, 86
Leveson-Gower, Lord Ronald
   Charles Sutherland, 77
Levy, Mr. Edward, 73
Lewis, Mr. George Henry, 76
Leyland, Captain Herbert
   Scarisbrick Naylor, 94
Lichfield, The Very Rev. Edward
   Bickersteth, Dean of, 84
Lichfield, The Bishop of, 97
Liddell, The Hon. Sir Adolphus
   Frederick Octavius, 82
Liddell, The Very Reverend Henry
   George, 75
Liddon, The Rev. Henry Parry, 76
Li Hsi, The Emperor of Corea, 99
Limerick, The Earl of, 85
Lincoln, Bishop of, 90
Lindley, Sir Nathaniel, 90
Lindsay, Col. The Hon. Charles
   Hugh, 82
Lindsay, Sir Coutts, of Balcarres,
   83
Lindsay, Lord, 78
Lindsay, James (see Crawford)
Lindsay, Col. Robert James Lloyd,
   76

Lipton, Sir Thomas Johnstone, 101
Liszt, The Abbe, 86
Lloyd, Mr. Edward, 92
Lloyd, Mr. Sampson S., 82
Loates, Sam, 96
Loates, Tom, 90
Loch, Sir Henry Brougham, 94
Locke, Mr. John, 71
Lockhart, General Sir William
    Stephen Alexander, K., 98
Lockwood, Colonel Amelius
    Richard Mark, 94
Lockwood, Mr. Frank, 87
Loder, Major Eustace, 106
Lodge, Sir Oliver Joseph, 104
Londesborough, Lord, 78
London, The Bishop of, 97
Londonderry, The Marquess of
    (Geo. Vane-Tempest), 76
Londonderry, The Marquess of
    (Chas. Vane-Tempest), 96
Long, Mr. Walter Hume, 86
Lonsdale, The Rt. Hon. The
    Earl of, 86
Lonsdale, The Earl of, 79,112
Lonsdale, Gladys, Countess, 83
Lopes, The Rt. Hon. Sir H.C.,93
Lopes, Sir Massey, 75
Loraine, Mr. Robert, 112
Lorn, The Marquis of, 70
Loti, Pierre (Julien Viaud), 95
Loubet, Emile, The President of
    the French Republic, 99
Louis, William Frederick, The
    King of Prussia, 71
Louisa, Victoria Adelaide
    Maria, Crown Princess of
    Germany and Prussia, 84
Lowe, Right Hon. Robert, 69
Lowell, Mr. James Russell, 80
Lowther, Hugh Cecil
    (see Lonsdale)
Lowther, The Rt. Hon. J.W.
    (The Speaker), 107
Lowther, The Rt. Hon. James, 100
Lowther, Mr. James, 77
Lowther, Mr. James William, 91
Lowther, The Hon. William, 81
Lubbock, Sir John, Bart., 78
Lubbock, Mr. Edgar, 106
Lucan, General The Earl of, 81
Lucas, Sir Arthur, 109
Lucas, Mr. John Seymour, 99
Luck, Lieut. Gen. Sir George,107

Lucy, Mr. H.W., 105
Lugard, Capt. Frederick John
    Dealtry, 95
Lumley, Mr. Augustus Savile, 74
Lumsden, Maj. Gen. Sir Peter
    Stark, 85
Lunn, Dr. H.S., 109
Lurgan, Lord, 92
Lush, The Hon. Sir Robert, 73
Lush, Mr. Justice M., 111
Lushington, Mr. Franklin, 99
Lusk, Alderman, 71
Lutteur III (horse), 109
Lyons, Sir Joseph, 110
Lyons, Lord Richard, 78
Lymington, Viscount, 80
Lyne, The Rev. Joseph Leycester,
    87
Lysons, Major-General Sir
    Daniel, 78
Lyttelton, The Hon. Alfred, 84
Lyttelton, Lord, 71
Lyttelton, The Rev. and Hon.
    Canon Edward, 101
Lyttelton, Gen. The Hon.
    Neville Gerard, 101
Lyttelton, The Hon. Spencer, 75
Lytton, The Earl of, 106
Lytton, Lord, 70,76

M

M'Arthur, Mr. William, Lord Mayor
    of London, 81
McAuliffe, Mr. W., 111
McCall, Mr. Robert Alfred, 103
McCalmont, Mr. H.L. Blundell, 96
McCalmont, Mr. Harry, 89
McCalmont, Maj.-Gen. Sir Hugh,106
McCarthy, Mr. Justin, 85
McDonnell, The Hon.
    Schomberg Kerr, 94
McEwan, Mr. William, 102
McIver, Sir Lewis, Bart., 96
McKenna, Mr. Reginald, 113
McKenna, Mr. Reginald, 106
McKinley, William, The President
    of the United States, 99
McLean, Mr. Douglas Hamilton, 97
McNeill, Duncan (see Colonsay)
Macara, Sir Chas. W., 112
Macclesfield, The Earl of, 81
Maclure, Mr. John William, 92
MacCormac, Sir William, 96
MacDona, Mr. John Cumming, 94

Michael Michaelovitch of Russia, The Grand Duke, 108
Michalovitch, The Grand Duke Michael, of Russia, 94
Middleton, Mr. Richard William Evelyn, 101
Middleton, Captain William George, 83
Midleton, Viscount, 76
Milbank, Mr. Frederick Acclom, 75
Miles, Sir Philip John William, 79
Mill, Mr. John Stuart, 73
Millais, Mr. John Everett, 71
Millar, Mr. Charles Gibson, 94
Miller, Sir James, 90
Milltown, The Earl of, 83
Milne, Sir Alexander, 82
Milner, Sir Alfred, 97
Milner, Sir Frederick George, 85
Milner, Mr. Marcus Henry, 90
Minoru (horse), 109
Minto, The Earl of, 105
Mitchell, Sir Henry, 90
Mitchell, Mr. Richard A.H., 96
Mitford (see Redesdale)
Moltke, Field-Marshal Count Von, 84
Monro, Mr. James, 90
Monsell, The Rt. Hon. William, 71
Montagu, The Hon. Oliver George Paulett, 77
Montagu, Lord Robert, 70
Montagu, Mr. Samuel, 86
Montagu, W.D. (see Manchester)
Montagu-Douglas-Scott, Lord Henry John, 81
Montgomery, Mr. Alfred, 78
Montrose, The Duke of, 82
Moody, Mr. Dwight L., 75
Moore, Mr. George, 97
Moore, H.F.S. (see Drogheda)
Moray, The Earl of, 98
Morgan, The Rev. Edmund Henry, 89
Morgan, The Hon. F.C., 93
Morgan, Mr. George Osborne, 79
Morgan, The Rev. Henry Arthur, 89
Morley, Mr. John, 78
Morley, Mr. Samuel, 72
Morley, Mr. Samuel Hope, 105
Morocco, The Emperor of, 91
Morris of Spiddal, Lord, 93
Morton, Mr. A.C., 93

Mosley, Sir Oswald, 98
Mott, Mr. Charles Grey, 94
Moulton, Mr. John Fletcher, 100
Mountcashell, The Earl cf, 83
Mowbray, The Rt. Hon. Sir John Robert, 82
Muck, Dr. Carl, 99
Muller, Frederick Maximilian, 75
Mundella, Mr. Anthony John, 71
Munster, Count George Herbert, 76
Munster, The Earl of, 82
Muntz, Mr. Philip Albert, 92
Muntz, Mr. Philip Henry, 75
Murchison, Sir Roderick Impey, 70
Murphy, Mr. John Patrick, 89
Murray, The Rt. Hon. Andrew, The Lord Advocate, 96
Murray, Gen. Sir James Wolfe, 105
Murray, John (see Athole)
Musurus Pacha, H.E., 71
Muttlebury, Mr. S.D., 90
Muzaffer-Ed-Din, The Shah of Persia, 103

N

Napier of Magdala, General Lord, 78
Napoleon III, 69
Nasser-Ed-Din-Shah, H.I.M. The Shah of Persia, 73
Nawab Nazim of Bengal, Behar, and Orissa, The, 70
Neeld, Colonel Audley Dallas, 100
Nelke, Mr. Paul, 108
Nelson, Earl (Horatio), 81
Nevill, Lady Dorothy, 108,112
Nevill, William (see Abergavenny)
Newdegate, Mr. C.N., 70
Newlands, Lord, 109
Newman, The Rev. John Henry, 77
Newnes, Mr. George, 94
Newry and Morne, Viscount, 76
Newton, Lord, 108
Newton, Mr. A.J.E., 93
Nicholas II, H.I.M. The Czar, K.G., 97
Nicholson, C.E., 113
Nickalls, Mr. Guy, 89
Nickalls, Mr. Thomas, 85
Nigra, Count C., 86
Nikisch, Arthur, 113
Noel, The Hon. Gerard James, 71
Norfolk, The Duke of, 81

Rances Y Villaneuva, Don
  Manuel, 71
Ranelagh, Viscount, 70
Ranjitsinhje, Jumar, Shri, 97
Rankin, Sir James, 113
Rasch, Major Frederic Carne, 96
Ravenscroft, Mr. Clarence, 111
Rawle, Mr. Thomas, 105
Rawlinson, Sir Henry Creswicke,
  73
Rawlinson, Mr. J.F.P., 108
Rawson, Vice-Admiral Sir Henry
  Holdsworth, 101
Rayleigh, Lord, 99
Read, Mr. Clare Sewell, 75
Read, Mr. John Francis
  Holcombe, 88
Read, Mr. Walter William, 88
Redesdale, Lord (Freeman-
  Mitford), 75,104
Redmond, Mr. John Edward, 92,104
Redwood, Sir Boverton, 108
Ree, Mr. Frank, 112
Reed, Mr. Edward James, 75
Rees, Mr. J.D., 107
Reeves, Mr. John Sims, 90
Regnart, Sir Horace, 109
Reid, Mr. Mayne, 73
Reid, Sir Robert Threshie, 95
Reid, Sir Robert Threshie, 113
Reid, Mr. Whitelaw, 102
Reiff, John, 100
Reiff, Lester, 100
Renan, Mr. Joseph Ernest, 79,110
Rendlesham, Lord, 81
Reszke, M. Jean De, 91
Reuter, Baron George De, 109
Reuter, Baron Paul Julius, 72
Revelstoke, Lord, 88,98
Rhodes, The Hon. Cecil, 91,98
Rhodes, Col. Francis William, 99
Rhys-Williams, 113
Ribblesdale, Lord, 81
Richard, Mr. Henry, 80
Richard, Hugo (see Elcho)
Richardson, Mr. Harry Leo Sydney,
  108
Richardson-Gardner, Mr. Robert,
  77
Richmond, The Duke of, 70
Rickaby, Fred, 101
Ridding, George (see Bishop
  Southwell)

Ridgeway, Edw.(see Bishop
  Kensington)
Ridley, Mr. Justice, 97
Ridley, Sir Matthew, 81
Ridley, Viscount, 110
Rigby, Sir John, 93
Rigby, Lord Justice John, 101
Rimington, Major Michael, 98
Ripon, The Bishop of, 106
Ritchie, Mr. Charles Thomson, 85
Robartes, Lord, 82
Roberts, Field Marshal Lord, 100
Roberts, Mr. John, Jr., 85,105
Roberts, Gen. Sir. F., 80
Roberts, Mr. Marshall, 111
Robertson, The Rt. Hon. Edmund,
  107
Robertson, Sir William Tindal, 89
Robins, The Rev. Arthur, 97
Robinson, Sir Clifton, 109
Robinson, Dr. J. Armitage, Dean
  of Westminister, 105
Robinson, Sir John, 111
Robson, Sir W.S., 106
Rochefort, Henri, 70
Rock Sand (horse), 109
Rocksavage, The Earl of, 83
Rodd, Mr. James Rennell, 97
Roden, The Earl of, 76
Rodin, M. Auguste, 104
Rodney, Lord Geo. B., 88
Roebuck, Mr. John Arthur, 74
Rogers, Mr. James Edwin
  Thorold, 84
Rollit, Sir Albert Kaye, 86
Romer, The Hon. Sir Robert, 91
Ronald, Landon, 113
Roosevelt, Mr. Theodore, President
  of the United States, 102
Rose, Mr. Charles Day, 104
Rose, Sir Philip, 81
Rose, Sir William, 85
Rosebery, The Earl of, 76,101
Rosslyn, The Earl of, 81
Rostand, M. Edmond, 101
Rothschild, The Lord Nathan, 88
Rothschild, Mr. Alfred De, 84
Rothschild, The Baron Alphonse De,
  94
Rothschild, Mr. Arthur De, 100
Rothschild, Baron Ferdinand
  James De, 89
Rothschild, Mr. Leopold De, 84

Rothschild, Baron Lionel Nathan
De, 77
Rothschild, Baron Mayer Amschel
De, 71
Rothschild, The Hon. Walter
Lionel, 100
Rous, Admiral, 70
Rous, John E.C. (see Stradbroke)
Rowe, Mr. George Duncan, 106
Roze, Raymond, 113
Ruggles-Brise, Sir Evelyn, 110
Ruskin, Mr. John, 72
Russell, Earl of, 69
Russell, The Hon. Mr. Charles,
107
Russell, Mr. Charles (of
Killowen), 83
Russell, Sir Charles, 78
Russell, Lieut.-Colonel Lord
Charles James Fox, 73
Russell, Sir Charles, 90
Russell, Sir George, 89
Russell, The Right Hon. Lord
Odo William Leopold, 77
Russell, Oliver (see Ampthill)
Russell, Mr. Thomas Wallace, 88
Russell, Mr. William Howard,
75
Rutherford, W.G., The Headmaster
of Westminster School, 98
Rutland, The Duke of, 71
Rutzen, Mr. Albert De, 100
Ryder, Dudley (see Harrowby)
Rylands, Mr. Peter, 79
Ryle, The Rt. Rev. John Charles,
Bishop of Liverpool, 81
Ryle, The Rev. E., 112

S

St. Albans, The Bishop of, 106
St. Albans, William Amelius,
Aubrey De Vere Beauclerk,
Duke of, 73
St. Simon (horse), 109
Sala, Mr. George Augustus, 75
Saldanha, The Duke of, 71
Salisbury, Marquis of, 69,100
Salomons, Sir David, 108
Salvini, Signor Tommaso, 75
Sambourne, Mr. Edward Linley, 92
Samuda, Mr. Joseph D'Aguitar, 73
Sandeman, Mr. Albert George, 95
Sanderson, Dr. John Scott
Burdon, 94

Sanderson, Sir Thomas Henry, 98
Sandhurst, The Rt. Hon. Lord,
74,89
San Giuliano, His Excellency The
Marquis Di, 108
Sankey, Mr. Ira D., 75
Santley, Mr. Charles, 102
Santry (horse), 110
Sarasate, Senor Pablo Martin
Meliton, 89
Sardou, M. Victorien, 80,91
Sargeant, Mr. John Singer, 109
Sassoon, Sir Albert Abdallah
David, 79
Sassoon, Sir Albert Edward, 100
Sassoon, Mr. Reuben, 90
Satow, Sir Ernest, 103
Saunderson, Col. Edw. J., 87
Savage-Landor, A. Henry, 113
Savage, Sir G.H., 112
Savile, Mr. Henry, 80
Savile, Lord John, 108
Savory, Mr. Alderman, 90
Saxe-Weimar, Prince Edward of,
75
Say, M. Jean Baptiste Leon, 80
Sceptre & Maid of Corinth
(horses), 109
Schenck, General Robert Cumming,
U.S.A., 75
Schlater-Booth, The Rt. Hon.
George, 74
Schnadhorst, Mr. Francis, 92
Schouvaloff, Count, 75
Schuster, Mr. Felix, 106
Scott, Sir John E. A. Murray,
109
Scott, Mr. Montagu David, 82
Scott, Capt. Percy, 103
Scott, Robert Falcon, 113
Scott-Gatty, Sir Alfred, 104
Scotter, Mr. Charles, 91
Scrutton, Mr. Justice, 111
Seafield, Earl of, 83
Searle, Henry, 89
Seddon, The Right Hon. Richard
John, 102
Seely, Mr. Charles, 78
Seely, Major John Edw., 105
Sefton, The Earl of, 94
Selborne, The Earl of, 101
Selby, James, 86
Selfridge, Mr. H. Gordon, 111
Selkirk, The Earl of, 82

Selous, Mr. Frederic Courtney, 94
Semon, Sir Felix, 102
Sewell, James E. Warden of
  New College, Oxford, 92
Seymour, Captain Conway, 84
Seymour, Sir Edward Hobart, 101
Seymour, Sir Francis, 77
Shackleton, Mr. Ernest, 109
Shaftesbury, Earl of, 69
Shand, The Baron Alexander, 103
Shaughnessy, Sir Thomas, 108
Shaw, Captain Eyre, 71
Shaw, Mr. George Bernard, 105, 111
Shearman, Mr. Montague, 95
Shelley, Sir Percy Florence, 79
Sheppard, The Rev. Canon Edgar, 111
Sheppard, The Rev. Edgar, 104
Shorter, Mr. Clement King, 94
Shrewsbury and Talbot, The
  Earl of, 103
Shrewsbury and Talbot, The
  Earl of, 80
Shuster, Mr. Morgan, 112
Shuttleworth, Colonel Frank, 109
Shuttleworth of Gawthorpe, The
  Rt. Hon. Lord, 104
Simmons, Sir John Lintorn
  Arabin, 77
Simon, Sir John, Sergeant-at-
  Law, 86
Simon, Sir John, 111
Simpson, Mr. Wm. Spiers, 110
Sinclair, Sir John George
  Tollemache, 80
Sinclair, Mr. W. Gardner, 109
Sing, The Mahraj Sir Pertab., 87
Singh, Duleep, His Highness
  The Maharajah, 82
Sivewright, Sir James, 93
Skelmersdale, Lord, 71
Slagg, Mr. John, 84
Slatin, Col. Sir Rudolf Carl, 99
Sloan, Tod, 99
Smiles, Mr. Samuel, 82
Smith, The Hon. Sir Archibald
  Leven, 88
Smith, Captain Arthur, 84
Smith, Sir Cecil Clementi, 92
Smith, The Rev. Ernest John
  Heriz, 88

Smith, Mr. F.E., 107
Smith, Mr. F.E, 111
Smith, Captain Malcolm Kincaid, 109
Smith, Samuel, 104
Smith, Mr. Richard Vassar Vassar, 110
Smith, The Hon. W.F.D., 104
Smith, Mr. William Henry, 72
Smith, The Rt. Hon. William
  Henry, 87
Smith-Dorrien, General H.L., 101
Sneyd, Mr. Ralph, 98
Soltykoff, H.S.H. Prince
  Demtrey, 89
Somerset, The Duke of, 69,93
Somerset, Major Lord Henry
  Arthur George, 87
Southampton, Lord, 107
Southwell, The Bishop of, 101
Soveral, Senhor Luiz De, 98
Soveral, The Marquess De, 107
Soveral, Marquis De, 112
Spencer, The Hon. C.R., 81
Spencer, Earl, 70
Spencer, Mr. Herbert, 79
Spencer-Churchill, Chas. (see
  Marlborough)
Spencer-Churchill, Lord Randolph
  Henry, 80
Spicer, Mr. Evan, D.L., 112
Spicer, Dr. Robert Henry Scanes, 102
Spofforth, Mr. Frederick Robert, 78
Spofforth, Mr. Markham, 80
Spooner, Mr. Reginald Herbert, 106
Spooner, Mr. W.A., 98
Sprigg, The Rt. Hon. Sir John
  Gordon, 97
Spurgeon, The Rev. Charles, 70
Staal, M. De, 85
Stainer, Sir John, 91
Stair, The Earl of, 83
Stanford, Sir Charles, 105
Stanhope, The Hon. Edward, 79
Stanhope, Peter (see Weardale)
Stanhope, Philip-Henry Stanhope,
  Earl, 74
Stanley, Very Rev. Arthur Penrhyn,
  Dean of Westminster, 72
Stanley, The Rt. Hon. Frederick
  Arthur, 79

Stanley, Mr. H.M., 72
Stanley, Lord, 69,94
Stansfeld, Rt. Hon. James, 69
Star(r), Mrs., 69
Steel, Mr., 77
Steele, Gen. Sir Thomas Montagu, 78
Stephen, Sir Alexander Condie, 102
Stephen, James Fitzjames, 85
Stephens, James, 113
Stephenson, Gen. Sir Frederick Charles Arthur, 87
Stepney, The Bishop of, 106
Stevens, Mr. Marshall, 110
Stevenson, H.W., 105
Stevenson, Dr. Thomas, 99
Stewart (see Marquis Londonderry)
Stewart, Gen. Sir Donald Martin, 87
Steyn, Mr. Martinus Theunis, 100
Stirling-Crawfurd, Mr. William Stuart, 79
Stirling, Mr. Justice James, 97
Stirling, Sir Walter George, 84
Stirling-Stuart, Mr. William Crawfurd, 104
Stoddart, Mr. Andrew Ernest, 92
Stone, Sir John Benjamin, 102
Stoll, Mr. Oswald, 111,113
Stone, John Benjamin, 102
Storks, Sir H.K.,70
Stracey, Lieut.-Colonel Henry, Scots Guards, 80
Stracey, Sir Henry Josias, 75
Stradbroke, The Earl of, 75
Straight, The Hon. Mr. Justice, 79
Strathcona and Mount Royal, The Lord, 100
Strathnairn, Lord, 70
Strauss, Herr Eduard, 95
Stuart, Alan P. (see Galloway)
Stuart, Mr. Douglas, 107
Stuart, E.A. (see Moray)
Stuart, Dr. James, 99
Stuart-Murray (see Tullibardine)
Stuart-Wortley, Mr. Archibald John, 90
Stuart-Wortley, Mr. Charles Beilby, 86
Stuart-Wortley, Maj. Edward James Montagu, 99

Stubbs, Charles (see Bishop Truro)
Sturge, Mr. E., 86
Sturt (see Alington)
Sturt, Col. Charles Napier, 76
Sturt, The Hon. Humphrey Napier, 92
Suffield, Lord, 79
Suffolk and Berkshire, The Earl of, 87
Suffield, Lord, 107
Sullivan, Mr. Arthur, 74
Sullivan, Sir Edward Robert, 85
Sumner, Hon. Charles, Member of the United States Senate, 72
Sutherland, The Duke of, 70
Sutherland, Mr. Thomas, 87
Sutton, Dr. Bland, 110
Swann, Mr. S.E., 112
Swinburne, Mr. Algernon Charles, 74
Swinton, Capt. C.S.C., 112
Sydney, Viscount, 69
Sykes, Mr. Christopher, 74
Sykes, Lieut.-Col. Mark, 112
Sykes, Sir Tatton, 79

T

Tadema, Mr. Laurence Alma, 79
Tailby, Mr. William Ward, 99
Tait, Rev. (see Canterbury)
Talbot, Edward, The Bishop of Rochester, 104
Talbot, The Rt. Rev. E.S., 111
Talbot, Mr. John Gilbert, 97
Talbot, Major-General The Hon. Reginald, 97
Tanner, Mr. Charles Kearns Deane, 88
Tate, Mr. Harry, 112
Tatlow, The Hon. Robert Garnett, 109
Tattersall, Mr. Edmund, 86
Taylor, John Henry, 106
Taylor, Col. The Rt. Hon. Thomas Edward, 74
Taylor, Mr. Tom, 76
Teck, H.S.H. The Duke of, 102
Teck, Major H.S.H. Prince Francis Joseph Leopold Frederick, Of, 102
Teck, Prince, 70
Tellegen-Lou, M., 113

142

143

Wellington, His Grace The Duke
of, 112
Wells, Mr. C.M., 107
Wenlock, Lord, 93
West, Sir Algernon Edward, 92
West, Mrs. George Cornwallis,
112
West, Colonel William Cornwallis,
92
Westbury, Lord, 69
Westminster, The Archbishop of,
93
Westminster, The Marquis of, 70
Westmoreland, The Earl of, 83
Whalley, Mr. George Hammond, 71
Wharncliffe, Lord, 75
Whistler, Mr. James Abbott
M'Neill, 78
Whitbread, Mr. Samuel, 95
White, General Sir George
Stuart, 100
White, Mr. Henry, 99
White, The Rev. Henry, 74
Whitehead, Mr. James, 89
Whitley, Mr. E., 80
Whitmore, Mr. Charles
Algernon, 101
Wiggin, Mr. Henry, 92
Wilberforce, Archdeacon, 109
Wilberforce, Samuel (see Bishop
Oxford)
Wilde, James (see Penzance)
Wilde, Mr. Oscar, 84
Wilde, Thomas (see Lord Truro)
Wilkinson, The Rt. Rev. George
Howard, Bishop of Truro, 85
Wilkinson, Sir Joseph, 102
Wilks, Dr. Samuel, 92
William, Prince Frederick, The
Crown Prince of Prussia, 70
William, H.R.H. The Crown Prince
of Germany, 105
Williams, Sir A. Osmond, 109
Williams, Mr. Hwfa, 91
Williams, Lord Justice R.L., 99
Williams, Mr. Montagu, 79
Williams, Colonel Owen Lewis
Cope, 78
Williams, Sir Roland Vaughan, 90
Williamson, Sir Archibald, 109
Williams-Wynn, Mr. Charles
Watkin, 79
Williams-Wynn, Sir Watkin, 73

Willoughby, Sir John Christopher,
84
Wills, Sir W.H., 93
Wills, Mr. Justice Alfred, 96
Wilmot, Sir Robert Rodney, 103
Wilson, Mr. Charles Henry, 85
Wilson, Mr. Christopher
Wyndham, 91
Wilson, Mr. Erasmus, 80
Wilson, Mr. Philip Whitwell, 111
Wilson, R.H.R. Rimington, 105
Wilson, Mr. Rivers, 78
Wilson, Sir Samuel, 85
Wilson, Woodrow, 113
Wilton, The Earl of, 73
Wimborne, Lord, 82
Winans, Mr. Walter, 93
Winans, Mr. Walter, 109
Winchester, The Bishop of, 101
Winchester, The Marquis of, 77,
104
Winchilsea and Nottingham, The
Earl of, 80
Wingate, Colonel Francis
Reginald, 97
Winn, Mr. Rowland, 74
Winterton, Earl, 108
Wippel, Mr. P.H. Pridham, 110
Witt, Mr. John Gyorge, 98
Wolf, Mr. Lucien, 111
Wolfe-Barr, Sir John, 105
Wolff, Sir Henry Drummond, 74
Wolseley, Sir Garnet J., 74
Wombwell, Sir George Orby, 74
Wood, Charles (see Halifax), 86
Wood, Brigadier-General Sir
Evelyn, 79
Wood, Mr. Henry J., 107
Wood, J. Hickory, 113
Wood, The Reverend Joseph, 99
Woodall, Mr. William, 96
Woodburn, James, 90
Woods, Mr. Samuel Moses James, 92
Wooton, Frank, 109
Workman, Mr. C. Herbert, 110
Wright, Mr. Justice, 91
Wrightson, Sir Thomas, 108
Wrottesley, Lord Arthur, 95
Wyke, Sir Charles Lennox, 84
Wynard, Captain Edward, 98
Wyndham, Charles, 114
Wyndham, Mr. George, 100
Wyndham, The Hon. Percy Scawen,
80